WARRIORS
AND WILDMEN

WARRIORS AND WILDMEN

Men, Masculinity, and Gender

STEPHEN WICKS

Foreword by B. Mark Schoenberg

BERGIN & GARVEY
Westport, Connecticut • London

Library of Congress Cataloging-in-Publication Data

Wicks, Stephen.
   Warriors and wildmen : men, masculinity, and gender / Stephen
Wicks ; foreword by B. Mark Schoenberg.
      p.   cm.
   Includes bibliographical references and index.
   ISBN 0–89789–454–5 (alk. paper)
   1. Men—Psychology.   2. Masculinity (Psychology)   3. Sex role.
I. Title.
   HQ1090.W52   1996
   305.31—dc20   96–3623

British Library Cataloguing in Publication Data is available.

Library of Congress Catalog Card Number: 96–3623
ISBN: 0–89789–454–5

First published in 1996

Bergin & Garvey, 88 Post Road West, Westport, CT 06881
An imprint of Greenwood Publishing Group, Inc.

Printed in the United States of America

@∞™

The paper used in this book complies with the
Permanent Paper Standard issued by the National
Information Standards Organization (Z39.48–1984).

10 9 8 7 6 5 4 3 2 1

Contents

Foreword

A lot of people who read this book will agree that books for and about men are decidedly worthwhile, but many others, men and women alike, are yet to be persuaded. The general feeling seems to be that men are as strong and resourceful as the phrase "I'm all right, Jack," suggests, and that they don't need studying. The first part of the equation is okay, but the second part is off base.

It goes without saying that the politics of gender have complicated our lives. Truth be told, I'm not sure it had to be this way at all. When Robert Louis Stevenson observed that "there is so much good in the worst of us, and so much bad in the best of us, that it behooves all of us not to talk about the rest of us," he could easily have been talking about activists on the distaff side of the sexual divide. Critics will argue that statements such as these are proof positive that I am sorely in need of consciousness-raising, but it's only the simple truth that arguments about gender roles and gender relations have made a lot of ordinary people extremely contrary. Relations between men and women have taken a pounding, often for the most pedestrian of reasons. From the tempest of the innocent gesture, like opening a car door, to the teapot of tribal rhetoric, the notion of the "level playing field" popping into mind, talking about the "rest of us" has become a tireless obsession. It is sad that the cult of the victim has become such a critical factor in the politics of gender. The author of this book tells us that "many women have been led to believe that any frustration or uncomfortable communication they experience at work is the result of a male environment that is naturally hostile to women." How better to position relations in the workplace? The English critic Charles Caleb Colton observed that each sex is a universal mirror to the other, that *the respective refinement of the one will be in reciprocal proportion to the other.* It seems clear that he believed that men bring out the best in women, and women the best in men. There are specific affective and behavioral dimensions to being male and there are specific affective and behavioral dimensions to being female, but differences per se do not make for inequality. Being a victim does!

The marginalization of men and masculinity is of great concern. Important elements of the media continue to be intrigued by the anti-male bias of the feminist agenda, and we have to do what we can to swim against this mainstream of populist thought. Clearly some men *are* bubbas and others *may be* bozos, but it's a bit much to tar all men with the same brush. That distinction is frequently lost on those who wield the power to decide what news gets reported, and the slant the article will take. The glass ceiling is a reality, but so is the velvet curtain; I would wager that you have heard more of the one than the other.

Some of the social consequences of marginalization are now beginning to appear, but it's likely that the full cost will not be known for another generation or two. Historically, attitudes and beliefs fall in and out of fashion, and this knowledge provides real hope that what goes around will truly come around. The coming together of the Promise Keepers and the initial success of the Million-Man March are hopeful signs that the turn around process has begun. But damage has been done, much of it by the oft repeated preachment that father's place is not necessarily in the home. Wicks tells us that "the strife of the urban ghetto is partly attributable to the disintegration of a male authority structure," and that "the alarming trend toward fatherless households is a societal powder keg." I agree, but selling the message is tough. The nature and size of the problem tends to render the average person confused, helpless, or apathetic. We are constantly reminded that education is the answer, but the question "whose education?" is by far the more important. The subject matter of this book serves to educate, but so do the sleaziest of talk-shows. Scary, isn't it? The bottom line is, we've got a lot of education to do.

Mr. Wicks has written a good book, and I am pleased to recommend it to you.

B. Mark Schoenberg, EdD
Professor Emeritus in Counselling
Memorial University of Newfoundland

Preface

Intense attention to women during the last three decades has raised important questions about how sex colors our consciousness and experience. Until recently, the focus of gender study has been almost exclusively on women's experience. Now men too have begun to realize just how powerfully gender influences their lives. Not only do men feel the need to understand what it means to be male, but they must pursue this goal in the shadow of an established feminist order that often condemns explorations of masculinity by men as part of a backlash against the social gains of women. These largely misguided attacks have impeded the growth of sex and gender study. As a result of the women's movement, current thinking on sex difference is dictated by feminist theory, and the concept of masculinity has not been studied in depth. Feminist attempts to unveil the deeper meanings of masculinity have perpetuated many myths, but offered little insight into the gender experience of men and sex difference in general. Predictably, then, most men and women are oblivious to the complex biological, psychological, and social factors associated with maleness, and only a small minority of astute men and women acknowledge the obstacles males face on the road to becoming men.

This book was inspired by the belief in a profound need to re-evaluate the presuppositions of feminist theories, especially the contemporary feminist view of men and masculinity. The marginalization of men and masculinity, I will argue, has allowed our understanding of human sex difference to stray into fallacy. Contemporary popular beliefs about men, women, and sex can seldom withstand the tests of logic and evidence. More frequently, such beliefs reflect distortions perpetuated to achieve political goals. While many historians correctly see the political and economic advancement of women as a great accomplishment, only a minority of social critics realize that the gains of women have incurred a certain cost to the gender economy that reverberates through all levels of our culture. This statement is not intended as a criticism of women's liberation per se, but rather as a caveat. So deeply rooted and pervasive is sex, that to attempt to subvert its energy radically and quickly by social arrangement is to tamper with nature itself, a potentially risky and ultimately futile endeavor.

There are two sexes. Only significant insight into *both* sexes will increase our understanding of both women and men and lead to a foundation of knowledge from which to draw as we attempt to better understand the problems of the sex-divide. Relationships between men and women, husbands and wives, fathers and children, and male and female friends will be better understood by both sexes as our growing knowledge of women is balanced by a better understanding of men.

What follows is an attempt at the long-overdue reevaluation of predominant ideas about men. The ideas are largely based on the work of prominent thinkers, both male and female, in a variety of disciplines who have rejected the prevailing notions of sex and gender.

This is a book about men. But, as feminism has shown, it is impossible to discuss aspects of one sex without frequently comparing and contrasting them with characteristics of the other. While the book is written about men by a man, it is written as much for women as for men. It speaks to the countless men confused about the shifting ideals of manhood. I hope that the ideas I present illuminate the factors that influence male identities, attitudes, and behaviors for such men, and that the same words offer women, particularly those dissatisfied with the notions of contemporary feminism, an alternate perspective from which to view men and their relationships with them. From the party-line feminist who chooses to read further, I merely request a fair hearing.

Every book is limited in what it can hope to integrate into the discussion of a particular subject. In this book, I do not elaborate on two themes that are frequently discussed in conjunction with gender: homosexuality and race. I believe these aspects of the subject deserve to be carefully and thoroughly studied. But in these pages I seek to isolate sex. I believe there are certain inherent differences between the sexes that limit the possibilities of social construction. These differences distinguish gender from race and class. An understanding of the theories I discuss is a prerequisite to studies of gender that consider additional factors such as race and class. Writing as a heterosexual male, I offer a heterosexual view of sexual relationships. I do not directly address the specific issues of gay men, or offer any opinion as to the origin of homosexuality, but I am confident that many gay men will be able to identify with many issues I address.

One final note about words. The terms "sex" and "gender" are often used interchangeably. Sometimes a distinction is drawn between them in which "gender" implies the socially attributed features of sex, and "sex" refers to obvious anatomical differences. Because I propose the idea that biological sex inevitably limits social arrangement, I use the terms more or less interchangeably.

This book is partly a product of my own struggle with manhood and identity. My research provided me with many answers but raised a whole new set of intriguing questions as well. This is precisely what I hope the reader will experience, an awakening to the complexities of the male condition that inspires deeper probings into the fascinating and puzzling realm of sex difference.

Acknowledgements

I could not have written this book without advice and encouragement from many people.

I express my deepest gratitude to my parents, Barbara and Ulrich Wicks, and my sister Elisabeth, for their unwavering support and helpful feedback throughout the process of researching and writing.

I am also indebted to many friends and colleagues who shared their experiences and opinions with me. I would especially like to thank Douglas Bost, Lisa Cesarani Kambolis, Mary Elizabeth Gorman, Vanessa E. Greenwood, Christopher Hatfield, B. Mark Schoenberg, and Edward Tang.

The editorial guidance I received from Jason Azze, Lynn Flint, Elizabeth Murphy, and Frances Rudner at Greenwood Publishing Group is greatly appreciated.

Introduction:
Studying Men and Masculinity

The truth of the matter is that nobody really, or naturally, likes to think about gender. Thinking about gender is irritating in the same way thinking about breathing or the beating of our hearts is irritating. We don't have to acquire a gender; we *are* gendered. In our deepest beings from the first, we are male or female. We discover this fact; we do not invent it. When we think about gender, that thinking is gendered.

Richard Hawley
Preface to *Boys Will Be Men* (xvii)

Gender has become a hot topic among scholars across all disciplines as well as among popular audiences. The controversy surrounding sex and gender alerts us to an increasing need to resolve the confusing state of gender affairs that now exists in our culture. But a great obstacle stands in the way of progressive thinking about sex difference. Hawley (1993) clearly conveys the main reason the sex dilemma seems impossible to decode: We have adopted a faulty line of thinking about gender. Perhaps because of human arrogance, most people believe that we can control nature, one of whose unavoidable features is sex. We are not taught to be male or female, we simply *are* male or female.

Hawley (1993: xix) elaborates on the degree to which we have taken the absurd notion that we can orchestrate sexual relationships by social arrangement.

Men and women are encouraged to be economically interchangeable parts. Work itself has become abstract and ultimately incomprehensible. The basis for loving sustained relationships, for families, has disappeared. In this modern arrangement, the very idea of gender, of innate gender, is a threat. There are commercial inducements to make a "unisex," to "blend" the genders, to make them equal in value, to make them meaningless.

If we continue on the current path of viewing gender as a threat, while nature continues to work its magic behind our backs, what will be the outcome? Hawley's conclusion warns of the risks we face if we continue to misinterpret the innateness of sex. While he does not specifically describe the damages that could be inflicted by our attempts to subvert nature's agenda, his warning is nonetheless sobering.

If gender really is deep and inalienable in our nature, it won't sit back quietly for long, much less disappear, if it is normed or legislated against. Like one of its offspring, sexuality, gender has the capacity to make fools out of individuals and of whole societies who get it wrong, either by undervaluing it, overvaluing it, or negating it (xx).

I have employed Hawley's words to emphasize that gender studies are over-reliant on social learning to account for differences in sexual behavior between men and women. While considerable evidence suggests that sex is an immutable force aligned with life itself, many of us educated in the wake of feminism have been led to believe otherwise. In the following chapter, I will offer evidence that supports the view Hawley and I share.

But let's briefly turn our attention to feminism, or more precisely, to the changing role of women during the twentieth century.

MEN IN THE WAKE OF FEMINISM

At the close of the last century a movement was afoot across the country to obtain political and economic equality for women. The suffragettes' movement began in an age when women could not vote and could be paid wages lower than those of men for the same jobs. With great difficulty, these politically imposed barriers, which systematically denied women equal social footing, were removed, and women began to assert their influence in areas once exclusively the domain of men. They proved that their sex was at least equally capable of performing traditionally male functions in an increasingly technological world. When several million American men answered the call to defend democracy during World War II, women filled the jobs they left behind. They assembled aircraft and ships, and manufactured ammunition. "Rosie the Riveter" became an icon of female strength in strenuous times. The surge of women into industry necessitated by World War II was the next most notable step toward women's economic independence and improved social standing after they were enfranchised by constitutional amendment in 1920.

Betty Friedan's *Feminine Mystique* appeared in 1963 and is considered the seminal work in an extensive feminist canon that continues to expand more than thirty years later. The issue of women's secondary status in society was a tangent of the civil rights movement that now exemplifies the Kennedy-Johnson years.

Later in that charged and pivotal decade, and continuing into the 1970s and 1980s, a new brand of feminism emerged. Attitudes toward men took on a distinctly unflattering quality. Males, in particular white males, became the scapegoat for women unhappy with certain aspects of our culture or their own lives.

There now exists a deeply entrenched feminist order in which men are routinely disparaged, fathers are marginalized in the context of families, and most of the undesirable situations in civilization can be blamed on men, or the imaginary conspiracy referred to loosely as "patriarchy."

Certain males have tended to blame or problematize women and femininity throughout history. Today's feminists, who point frequently to this fact, are guilty of advancing a similarly misguided premise. Now, however, it is men who are abnormal, spiritually inferior, and who keep the human race from reaching its full potential. The very language of pro-feminist literature speaks condescendingly of "humanizing" men, as if to suggest that women are the norm for human beings and that men are aberrant.

It seems safe to say that in the United States, on the eve of a new century, that the meanings of masculinity and the criteria for manhood are ambiguous at best. At worst, they are in critical disarray, and their deterioration may have far-reaching social consequences.

Masculinity has suddenly become a hot topic partly because of the need to respond to the widespread assault on men. Work has begun, and there is room for optimism: The 1990s witnessed an open questioning of the beliefs of feminism. Men are raising their voices and sharing their feelings after a generation-long period of silence. At their side are perceptive, open-minded women, disillusioned and frustrated with the political engine driving women's studies and the antimale attitudes that pervade feminist theory.

It is worth mentioning that without the challenges presented by feminism and the changing roles of women, the current wave of concern about men and masculinity might never have risen, and a ripe opportunity to better understand the essence of gender may have been missed. At a time when men as a group are under fire from all angles, a hard gaze into the workings of the male mind, intimidating as it may be at times, is a necessary task.

The extent to which gender studies span disciplines indicates how powerful a force they are. In Morgan's (1992: vii) words, gender is "the most pervasive and taken-for-granted feature of our lives. It figures strongly in the make-up of all societies." This very nature of gender, Morgan continues, is what makes problematic, "in terms of power, oppression, inequality, i and self-doubt." The terms Morgan lists surface in the work of the historian, the economist, the anthropologist, the linguist, the philosopher, the literary critic, the sociologist, and the psychologist. Gender is most visibly popular in the humanities and social sciences. But even the chemist and the biologist concern themselves with sex research in their much-publicized attempts to unlock the secrets of the brain, measure the effects of hormones, and translate the perplexing language of genetics.

WHY STUDY MEN?

How would it help us to know more about the way men think and behave? The possible applications of knowledge about masculinity are immensely diverse. We might consult available knowledge about men if we're trying to account for the distressing problem of violence in the inner city. A woman trying to gain the interest of a man in whom she's interested might want more insight into the way her potential partner sees her.

Domestic violence could be called the issue of the day. In our "fix-it-after-it-breaks" culture, we recognize the serious problem of marital abuse, fund shelters for women who have been battered, and seek to inflict harsher punishments on the offenders. Men's studies, by exploring the nature of the male psyche, could offer insight into what drives a man to the point of becoming an abuser. Knowing this, professionals would be able to reduce significantly the number of marital disputes in which a woman ends up injured, a man ends up behind bars, and both endure mental torments. For the benefit of both sexes, men should have access to information about the unique psycho-dynamics of forming male identity.

Our everyday exchanges stand to be improved by greater understanding of the male world. Communication between the sexes, whether at work, over a checkout counter, or in the throes of passion, depends on knowing how men's and women's minds function differently as well as how they function similarly.

One of the most deeply entrenched barriers to a clear understanding of gender dynamics stems from the widely held assumption that history, because it is filled with the deeds and creations of men, is also the history of masculinity. We know about Ho Chi Minh, Neil Armstrong, Michelangelo, Jesus Christ, and Dr. Martin Luther King, Jr. because their thoughts and actions transformed the world we live in and they have been immortalized in our collective consciousness. The deeds of famous men, artists, scientists, soldiers, clergymen, and criminals, do not necessarily provide a realistic and coherent picture of the male mind. Vastly outnumbered by men in the chronicles of human civilization, women appear overlooked in history. But men have been history's "ungendered" sex in the sense that records of men as men, as gendered beings, are scarce.

Looking at the details of history from the new perspective of men's studies, we have at our disposal an inexhaustible supply of examples of men as human beings who are struggling with their masculinity. Filene (1987:110-11) introduces us to such a case.

Because fathers were banished to the waiting rooms of history, we do not know how much they valued children. . . .in the course of Lincoln Steffen's famous *Autobiography* (1931) we encounter the author in many roles and many places. We meet the California Boy who galloped between deviltry and penitence; the young journalist who muckraked city bosses in the United States and then the Allied leaders in postwar Versailles. In this exuberant story a reader cannot detect, because Steffens himself did not fully admit, that a deep emotional frustration churned beneath the surface of his life. "My wife died and then her mother. A short sentence that, but it covers a long story." That it is all he told his public audience. In private letters, by contrast, he confessed that his marriage had "been barren for years." "I need a home," the lonely widower wrote plaintively to his sister. We are hardly astonished by this discrepancy between the public and private versions.

How fascinating it would be to investigate the psychodrama of

Steffen's life as a man, his nagging isolation and personal pain, and attempt to draw connections between his personal and professional lives. I predict that such studies will comprise a sizable category of scholarship on men.

QUESTIONS: WHAT DO WE NEED TO KNOW ABOUT MEN AND MASCULINITY?

What do we need to know in order to properly analyze past and present conditions and make progress toward alleviating the problems associated with masculinity, both individually and socially? What are we searching for when we peer below the surface of gender and into the sphere of masculinity? First we must decide what the critical questions are. The list of questions we can ask about men and masculinity indicates just how little we know about why men are the way they are. Below is a list, by no means exhaustive, of what I believe are the most pressing questions related to men and masculinity.

Are women really more oppressed than men by our social system?

Is there really a male conspiracy (patriarchy) in place that keeps women from attaining high-status employment and politically powerful positions?

Is all of history the story of men?

Why have there been so many more male physicists, architects, composers, inventors, artists? Is it because men have prevented women from excelling in these fields?

Why are men so much more prone to violence than women?

Why are men so fearful of expressing emotions in intimate relationships?

Why do men pursue sex more ardently than women?

Why do they shy away from commitment and express an interest in multiple partners?

Why does pornography appeal almost exclusively to men?

Without further delay, let us now seek some possible answers to these and other questions, which promise a more resolute picture of the intricate relationships among masculinity, sex, personal identity, and society.

1

Nature's Exiles: Psychobiology and The Male Predicament

Feminists often vilify a nebulous evil called "Patriarchy," and scholars ruminate about other social constructs, such as capitalism, as they attempt to account for the oppression of women. Feminist ideology has led gender scholarship astray by over emphasizing social arrangement in the analysis of male and female social behavior. Socialization and environment profoundly shape us, but these elements act only upon predetermined characteristics of which biological sex is one of the most obvious. Biology does not necessarily dictate an unchangeable destiny. But sexual freedom as an androgynous state in which biological sex is of no personal or social consequence is an unattainable ideal belonging to the realm of science fiction rather than reality.

The current climate of political correctness is resistant to the notion that physiological factors influence human behavior. The "nature or nurture" controversy has become more heated in recent years. Human consciousness, behavior, and social structure are almost certainly products of nature *and* nurture. What is hardwired into the psyche can be altered by social design, but only to a limited degree and never without consequence.

Physiological sex differences deserve far greater attention than many scholars working in gender studies and the social sciences have afforded. Our social environment is a consequence of our natural circumstances. In his famous seventeenth-century essay, *Of Nature in Man,* Francis Bacon (1985: 118-19) wrote that nature must be obeyed in order to be understood. Nature, Bacon said, is "often hidden, sometimes overcome, and seldom extinguished."

In *The Inevitability of Patriarchy,* Steven Goldberg (1977: 104-105) demonstrates the limitations of social influence on human behavior.

Socialization is limited by the observation of physical or behavioural manifestations of psychophysiological factors, and it is these limits which concerns us. Even if it were possible for socialization to ignore the psycho-physiological reality—and for children to be socialized to believe that fathers were not dominant and tall, mothers not nurturant and short—the psychophysiological factors responsible for these realities would still be at work and fathers would still be dominant and tall and mothers nurturant and short. . . .While the sociologist is quite correct in seeing parents as the agents who transmit societies' values to children, the mother who tells her eight-year old daughter that fighting is unladylike is not primarily concerned with transmitting societies' values but with preparing her daughter for a world in which fighting *is* unladylike (i.e. fighting is usually done by men), and in which her daughter, who might do quite well in fights against boys of her own age, will be at a big disadvantage if fighting ranks high among the methods with which she hopes to cope with adult life. In real life, most parents want to prepare their children for the real world, and are unwilling to sacrifice them to the demands of ideology—which is what they do when they grossly misrepresent the world and leave their children unprepared for life—even if such a sacrifice were not, for the reasons mentioned above, doomed to failure.

The purpose in stressing the power of psycho-physiology is not to make a case for male or female superiority. There is tremendous variation among men and tremendous variation among women. Moral and intellectual competence, as well as fallibility, are not specifically sex-related. There are, however, tendencies attributable to each sex that should not go unexplained. Our perceptions and the resultant behaviors often differ radically depending on our sex. Physiological distinctions, even the most evident ones, exert force on our consciousness. Why can't a man be more like a woman? This is the nagging question which I will now attempt to answer.

Men know they are sexual exiles. They wander the earth seeking satisfaction, craving and despising, never content. There is nothing in that anguished motion for women to envy (Paglia 1991:19).

Much has been made of the obstacles women face in achieving self-esteem and personal fulfillment. These obstacles are assumed to be imposed by a male-dominated social system. I propose that men, due to biological circumstance, are caught in a peculiar situation which I will refer to as the male predicament.

Masculinity is unstable and angst-ridden. In sharp contrast to femininity, masculinity depends entirely on an external definition. To a degree, the external anatomical structure and transitory biological role burden every man with a sense of vulnerability. I am inclined to believe that much of women's confusion and frustration about men arises from the fact that women take their sexual identity for granted. Nothing is more telling of this general incomprehension of the male predicament than questions such as, "Why can't men be more like women?"

Walter Ong (1989: 98) precisely illustrates the physical differences between men and women and hints at their powerful influences on the mind and human interaction.

A male finds his masculinity in some way outside of himself. . . . Masculinity is difficult to interiorize, a kind of stranger to the human psyche. Since being human means living from interiority, masculinity is an especially acute problem for human beings. . . .A certain anatomical externality is obvious in the male sexual organs. . . .The male finds himself anatomically entered in contest, on trial, having to call witnesses to give testimony as to what he actual is, not a woman, to "say" that he is a man. This situation is one of the deep manifold paradoxes of human existence.

Ong's explanation of male externality seems straightforward enough. But it isn't until male anatomy is contrasted with female anatomy that the true difference and its powerful influence on identity formation becomes apparent.

Woman's body is a mystery, for what is most distinctively feminine about it, its reproductive equipment is largely invisible. . . .Male sexual organs are not secret and mysterious: they are external, for everyone to see, and make fun of, often enough. The phallus and testicles are regularly the subjects of jokes, female organs more rarely and the womb almost never. . . In a profound sense, by contrast to man, woman is interiority, self-possession. . .[men's secrets] are weak and even ludicrous by comparison. They are manufactured secrets, imitations of women's natural secrets, calculated to establish males as distinct from women . . . .deep down, the men know that they have no real secrets at all.

The trauma of complete exposure, of having no secrets, goes a long way in accounting for male behavior. Unable to internalize his identity, an act that stabilizes and fixes one's idea of self, the human male has no choice but to seek meaning through inter-action with the external world. Masculinity is in constant view, subject to appraisal from without.

As a result of the need for external evidence of self worth, achievements for many men resemble water poured into a leaky vessel. Each success slowly drains away and another must take its place. A man typically comes to view success as that which he has not yet achieved. As Willard Gaylin pronounces in *The Male Ego:* "There are no successful men." This nagging reality holds true for the high school athlete, the mail-room clerk, and the mil-lionaire Wall Street bonds trader. The obsessive striving to create existential meaning externally has driven countless men to work themselves into early graves, as a man's job easily becomes his whole identity and existence. Women's evaluation of men in terms of their occupations fuels the work obsession. A fear women commonly express is that a man will leave her for a younger or more attractive woman. The comparable male fear is that the woman a man loves will run off with a wealthier or more socially successful man. In short, women's anxieties about whether their appearance measures up are comparable to the insecurity many men feel about the prestige and earning power of their jobs.

The application of different standards to men and women is often mistakenly attributed to social convention. Customs do not materialize from thin air; we must probe their origins, which often reside in our biology. While society may judge a man by his livelihood more or less harshly in various cultures and in different historical eras, the determinants that make such a measurement possible and probable reside in the structure of the male body itself.

THE PRENATAL ORIGINS OF THE MALE PREDICAMENT

All fetuses begin as female. Only the introduction of male sex hormones, known as androgens, signals the fetus to become male. Whether a female or male baby will be created depends on the chromosomal message delivered by the sperm cell. As the biology student knows, all ova are signified by "X" while all sperm are either "X" or "Y." If a sperm (X) penetrates the egg, the child conceived will be female (XX). If a sperm (Y) wins the race, a male child (XY) will be conceived. In the latter case, the fetal structures that would become a woman's ovaries instead develop into testes, which produce testosterone. Testosterone, more than any other hormone, significantly alters the pre-natal development of certain body structures (Wilson, 1992:28).

Even in the womb, a male must *become* male; in order for a boy to exist at all, an additive is required. Male exclusion from the cycles of nature begins at conception; a male will always need an extra element to substantiate his sexual identity.

MEN AS OUTCASTS IN THE REPRODUCTIVE CYCLE

Sexual physiology places men in an inferior sexual position to women. The well-known Freudian idea, that a woman is a castrated man, reveals less about the natural imbalance between male and female than a variation on this perspective: A man is a barren woman.

A woman receives monthly sexual affirmation through menstruation. Pregnancy and breast feeding, as well, remind a mother of her indispensable role in the perpetuation of life. Her entire body, with its life-creating potential, is an undeniable symbol of her significance and power. The male does not enjoy such continual reassurance. Intercourse is the only male sex act. A man's potency is the only evidence of participation in the reproductive process he can offer. Even then, the father's biological contribution to the creation of new life is transitory at best. To a certain degree, male sexual urgency and female restraint can be attributed to the greater repertoire of sex-affirming activities available to the female. A woman is far less dependent on sexual activity to construct and affirm her sexual identity.

The emotional devastation of male impotence stems from the demand for male sexual performance as proof of ability to participate in the mysterious process of creating life. Male sexual arousal is a prerequisite to sexual union, and thus to the propagation of the human species through normal reproduction. A woman is not under the same pressure. Neither the female's capacity to engage in sex nor her ability to conceive hinges on her level of interest or her performance. Intercourse, then, is an affirmation, though a painfully transitory one, of a man's masculinity. The conjugal act for a woman involves permitting access to a sacred, secret space. She governs the sexual province through granting or denying access to her hidden, protected interior. Thus, "every sex act is the result of female grant or male seizure" (Gilder 1973: 21). Society frowns upon female promiscuity, not solely because of a culturally imposed male prerogative, but because female identity "escapes" through the act of intercourse; a secret is momentarily compromised. Male sexual indiscrimination sustains an illusion of male biological usefulness and is more apt to be tolerated by men and women alike. Obviously, social mores reinforce this anatomical set up.

Through science, man has made himself even more dispensable in the procreative process. Artificial insemination, as proponents of a woman-only feminist utopia point out, allows a man who isn't even alive to become a (biological) father. Not only can a child be born posthumously, as countless babies have been since earliest humanity, but it is possible to conceive a child posthumously. Until science creates a substitute for the human womb, women need never confront such harsh exclusion from the reproductive cycle. Human males, take note: Our plight could be dimmer. In a blatant display of her sexual superiority, the female praying mantis not only kills but ingests her male partner *during* copulation. Among spiders, the female of several species stuns or kills the male for future use as food. Of course, our focus here is on the realm of human beings.

Perpetually unsure of their significance within the human family, men must create and defend their sense of masculinity. While a woman's inborn potential and sense of secret privilege anchor her identity, male psychic energy is raw, undefined, existent only when externalized. Consciously and unconsciously, he sees himself as an outcast. He knows that in order to approximate sexual equality with women, he must achieve, build, or create. Anxiety about his precarious position fuels his drive—sometimes to ridiculous or dangerous extremes—to become a man.

Numerous examples from literature and popular culture demonstrate the extremities and absurdities of the male quest for identity. Cervantes' Don Quixote, the impossible romantic who jousts windmills astride a donkey in his makeshift helmet, is archetypically male. No woman would engage in such futile pursuits (Ong 1989:99). How unlikely seems the prospect of a female Hamlet? The great animated tricksters, like the scheming Wile E.

Coyote and the super-mischievous Bugs Bunny, are almost always male.

CROSSING THE PSYCHIC ABYSS: REIDENTIFICATION WITH FATHER

Children of both sexes begin life with a close bond to their mother. As a child matures, self-confidence and self-sufficiency slowly supplant the mother's constant, life-sustaining care. For a girl, this journey is a relatively unbroken progression. She need not detach from her mother to find a suitable model for her gender identity. The young boy, on the other hand, faces a more complicated ordeal. His identity further depends on a separation from his mother and a successful reattachment to a suitable male role model. Traditionally, this would be the child's biological father.

Girls learn that they are like their mothers sexually. The formation of their identity is based on attachment. Boys cannot say that they are like their fathers without first realizing that they are what their mother is not. Separation forms the basis for their search for sexual identity. Masculinity, then, has its origins, both physiologically and psychologically, in a sense of anti-femininity (Kilmartin, 1994: 73).

For the developing young man, motion into the psychic abyss between parents is fraught with risk and confusion:

Disidentification does not occur in an instant. . . .Rather [the boy] begins. . .a process that will take years and contains many false starts and hair-pin turns. [M]en, in a burst of insecurity about their masculinity, wonder whether they are too womanly, in other words, too much like their mothers (Kupers 1993: 52).

At the same time that the boy begins to reject his mother and all things feminine, he still seeks her approval and remains dependent on her to some extent. A life long conflict begins that will compel a man to seek the acceptance of women, whom he depends upon to validate his manhood, while fearing and avoiding intimacy. Consider the young boy's reaction to a girl's kiss. His melodramatic show of disgust and indignation, which adults often find charmingly comic, is largely a protest against the affectionate contact that he associates with his mother.

Avoidance of intimacy and discomfort with emotion, two male qualities that every woman who has been intimately involved with a man knows well, are deeply rooted in the male predicament. Emotion opposes rationale. Rationale and outside conceptualization support the rickety scaffold of masculine self image. Emotional exposure is anathema to the male self. For a man to risk emotional exposure is to risk annihilation. Gaylin (1992:102) explains how routinely this vulnerability can be overlooked or misinterpreted by women.

A woman may assume that a man will be comforted by having the person who loves him recognize his vulnerability. She can then indicate that, coward or no, her love for him endures; physical courage is not important to her. Nothing could be more disastrous. Men generally do not respond well to conversations whose substance is: "Don't feel you have to pose, I know you're afraid and it's all right with me, I understand." It is they, the men, who will not understand. And to protect their pride they must deny their fear. Since the inevitable result of denied fear is rage, it will often be the woman who is assaulted.

Girls do not undertake a process of denying things masculine; they may remain assured in their girlhood without rejecting the opposite sex. The tolerance of tomboys by other children, both male and female, is noticeably greater than acceptance of the sissy or, to use the more revealing epithet, a "mama's boy."

But the boy's need to switch tracks is profound. The relationship between a boy and his father, or lack of it, will influence his success and security in all of his adult relationships. Deprivation of a father or a suitable male role model can have a devastating effect on individual growth. It seems probable that blatant homophobia and general devaluation of women can frequently be blamed on a particularly troublesome or unsuccessful break from identification with the mother and reidentification with a caring and reasonably stable male figure. Fear and insecurity about one's masculinity are strongly implicated in the loutish posturing of the misogynist.

On a large scale, Father Hunger, to borrow the mythopoetic term, can set the stage for social disaster. A boy without a father has only the trial-and-error approach through which to learn appropriate male behavior. Boys need men to make the rules and provide direction, to set limits. Single mothers of adolescent sons will be the first to tell you how difficult it is to make and enforce rules with no male authority figure present. But among the general population the need for male moral authority is seldom recognized, even though it is reasonably clear that in communities where appropraite male role models are scarce, crime rates highest. Such an obvious connection impels us to reconsider how the absence of a male authority figure in the formative years of a boy's life contributes to criminal behavior.

A complex interaction of psychological, social, racial, and economic factors is to blame for the explosion in the number of single-parent households in which boys are deprived of an adequate father. The devaluation of men and the implied disposability of fathers, ideas that taint popular thinking, unquestionably contribute. Regardless of causes, the alarming trend toward fatherless households with male children is a societal powder-keg.

Much recent conversation has centered on men's willingness to participate more actively in child rearing. Based on what I've just discussed, there's no question that a father plays an important role in his child's development. While paternal guidance seems especially crucial for sons, it is worth noting that daughters in homes without fathers are twice as likely to become pregnant out of wedlock and before age eighteen.

Sadly, feminization of the family has placed greater value on the nurturing care most often provided by mothers, at the expense of equally useful qualities, such as stability in the face of crisis, that are usually associated with fathers.

A mother's authority over her children derives from the

irrevocable fact that she has given birth to them. She does not feel threatened, as men do, that her authority can be easily undermined. It is much easier to reject the father, who cannot claim paternity of his children unless their mother allows him to. For this reason, the transferral of maternal duties to the father neither reduces the mother's responsibility nor necessarily provides the father with an adequate foundation of his masculinity. The fact that men have not subscribed to the idea of the new nurturing-father, as indicated by the complaints of women who work outside the home and who still end up with the greater share of household chores, is attributable to factors other than male selfishness. The hesitancy on the part of some fathers to contribute equally to nurturing child-care tasks may stem from the underlying insecurity that their efforts will not likely be recognized with same respect and reverence that the mother will receive for performing essentially the same duties.

MOZART AND JACK THE RIPPER: EXTREMES OF MASCULINITY

"There are no female Mozarts because there are no female Jack the Rippers," wrote Camille Paglia, one of many bold lines that infuriated the feminist mainstream. Feminists, not without abundant evidence, have identified violence as a male problem. Unfortunately, few theorists offer much in the way of rational explanations for the greater male propensity to violence. Men are simply impossible to civilize, asserts the sweeping rhetoric. The same critics hastily attribute the irrefutable historical record of a male majority among artists and scientists to a male conspiracy to suppress female achievement. Almost any feminist would argue that Attila the Hun, Hitler, Stalin, or any perpetrator of widespread human misery, could only have been male. But, should you suggest that Thomas Edison, Leonardo DaVinci, or the Beatles could only be men, the chances of agreement are slim. Feminists have tried to have it both ways, attributing violence to male moral inferiority but blaming male domination of the cultural realm to sexism. Wilson (1992: 98-99) clarifies for us why social theories are unsatisfactory to explain sex difference in cultural achievement:

Many male geniuses have had to override considerable disadvantage in their educational or social background. . . before their contributions are recognized. . . .Isaac Newton came from a family of small farmers, was a premature child so puny and weak he was not expected to live and received a poor education at the local village school. . . .Richard Wagner had virtually no musical training but taught himself harmony by buying a book in his late teens. . . .George Washington Carver emerged from a background of civil war and slavery in Missouri to become one of America's greatest biological scientists, despite constant hunger, poverty and ill health and having been denied an education because of his color . . . girls are given more than equal encouragement to learn music at school. . . .For hundreds of years, European ladies have been expected to sing and play an instrument such as the piano as a social grace, and yet the great composers have without exception been men.

One accounting of the preponderance of both high genius and the greater propensity toward criminality among men points to the chromosomal patterns I discussed earlier, in which (XX) represents the chromosomal pattern for the female, while the male is represented by (XY). Because women have two of the same chromosomes, each X acts as a "back-up" for the other. A faulty gene in one (X) may compensated for by the other (X). The fact that both extremes, genius and criminality, are more often found among men, results from the greater probability that something can go genetically haywire. Wilson (1992:108) explains "There are more men at the bright and dull ends of the spectrum. This apparently occurs because the second X chromosome in women has an averaging effect, canceling out extreme tendencies based on the other."

Chromosomes may indeed influence the higher incidence of both freak high intelligence and sociopathic behavior among men. But genius or substantial achievement in the arts and sciences cannot be attributed to intelligence or brain structure alone. Differences in intelligence stemming from chromosomal patterns are likely not the primary reason for the irrefutable fact of male domination of many areas of cultural achievement. It is the lack of natural grounding that compels men to persevere against considerable odds in hopes of defining themselves that is most responsible for the controversial history of male achievement.

Both extreme genius and criminality, with rare exception, are manifestations of the volatile energy born of the male predicament. It is man's vain efforts to extricate himself from the futility and isolation of his condition that we can thank for the most abstract scientific theories, and on which we can blame the terror of the serial killer. Violence, too, stems from this outward search for meaning, which women are not condemned to undertake. I will not fully address the question of why certain males become superb artists and scientists while others abuse, murder, and destroy. Biochemical influences and social conditions are almost certainly at play in determining such contrasting expressions of the same dilemma. An investigation of such influences deserves a separate volume in itself.

Highly critical of the feminist views that male domination is a result of oppression, Camille Paglia (1991:19-20) explains the relationship between culture and masculinity with unusual clarity:

Man is sexually compartmentalized. Genitally, he is condemned to a perpetual pattern of linearity, focus, aim, and directedness. . . .Men are out of balance. They must quest, pursue, court, or seize. . . .Women have conceptualized less in history not because men have kept them from doing so, but because women don't need to conceptualize in order to exist.

Paglia recognizes the true displacement and isolation of the male predicament. Left-wing scholars, who bemoan the scarcity of female artistic masterpieces and technological contributions fail to recognize the intrapsychic strife that fuels creation of such magnitude.

Projection is a male curse: forever to need something or someone to make oneself complete. This is one of the sources of art and the secret to its historical domination by males. The artist is the closest man has come to imitating women's superb self-containment. The blocked artist, like Leonardo, suffers tortures of the damned. The most famous painting in the world, the Mona Lisa, records woman's self-satisfied apartness, her ambiguous mocking smile at the vanity and despair of her many sons (Paglia 1991: 28).

In addition to physiology, the success or failure of the transitions from mother-identification to father-identification at an early age may compound a boy's sense of isolation from the emotional world of real people. Perhaps an overly possessive mother, or an abusive or absent father complicates the psychological development of some men. Such men feel rejection or helplessness and dependence to a greater degree than a boy who made a less troubled transition. This may spawn unusual achievement under one set of circumstances or heinous criminality under another. Men whose early interpersonal relationships are particularly fraught with pain retreat into a sphere of abstraction and analytic formality in which complex conceptualization is both possible and necessary. This seems to be the case with many renowned physicists and philosophers. David Thomas (1993: 44) offers one explanation for the behavior of some celebrated male theoreticians.

Having learned at an early age that profound feelings toward other people carry with them a profound emotional cost. . . .[They] choose to direct their emotions toward non-threatening targets. . . .[They] are often fascinated by abstract concepts, rather than human ones. . . . [N]umber, note, or particles are predictable, beautiful, and unable to cause pain. Men of extreme genius—including Newton, Descartes, Schopenhauer, Tolstoy, Kierkegaard, Goethe, Ruskin, and George Bernard Shaw—share a common desire to retreat from human intimacy in the direction of formality and abstraction. They tend too, to be sexless since sexual activity, with its threat of engulfment by women, is too painful to contemplate. . . .Newton, Locke, Pascal, Spinoza, Kant, Nietzsche, Wittgenstein, you could fill an encyclopedia. . .with the names of men whose children were their ideas, rather than any human offspring.

The very great majority of us are neither fascist dictators nor Nobel laureates. But these exceptional images illuminate the psychic forces that reside in every man producing various outcomes. Most men, though they are not theoretical physicists, world-famous painters, or brutal maniacs, will recognize in themselves elements of the male predicament.

With an understanding of the psycho-biological origins of masculinity, we can now turn to social factors and their role in shaping male identity.

2

The Ungendered Sex: The History and Sociology of Masculinity

Because of the amorphous sexuality of males, they must be given specific and exclusive tasks, not to accomplish the business of society, but to accomplish and affirm their own identities as males. If such roles are not given them, they disrupt the community, or leave it.

George Gilder
Sexual Suicide (1973: 84)

A BRIEF HISTORY OF MASCULINITY

Man the Hunter

The development of hunting among early humans served not only as a means of obtaining food but also provided the necessary division of labor in an increasingly complex society. Perhaps the longest-standing personification of manhood in our historical imagination is the pre-historic hunter.

Homo Erectus, who emerged about 1 million years ago, distinguished himself from earlier primates in that meat constituted a large portion of his diet. He was, however, a scavenger rather than a hunter. Numerous anthropological accounts indicate that it was Australopithecus who formed the first truly cooperative hunting groups. A mere 70,000 years ago, Neanderthal became skillful enough to bring down the legendary mammoth. Many early hominids subsisted without meat, and subsequent generations of primitive man seemed to have consumed meat as a supplementary, rather than a primary food source. Certainly, advancements in tools and weaponry and the harnessing of fire made hunting more viable, but it seems likely that our ancient male predecessors, groping for meaning and anxious to define themselves as distinct from women, found a manly niche in the ceremony of the hunt.

Women remained close to the hearth in early societies; they fulfilled child-rearing needs of the group, but their tasks were hardly limited to caring for young. Women, with their revered child-bearing powers, also presided over the mysteries of birth, life and death, and often filled the role of medicine women. As the gatherers in the hunter-gatherer society, women's contributions to the food supply were significant, and they also provided the items used for medicinal and ritual purposes. As they have in every society since, primitive men found it necessary to establish a contrasting role through which to define themselves; adequate definitions of masculinity are a prerequisite to the smooth functioning of a human social system.

Hunting as a means of survival, which it must have occasionally been, was certainly not constant or universal. Peter Stearns (1990:20) describes how hunting became inherently ritualistic, a practice based on proving one's masculinity:

As almost self-created hunters, physically feeble save for their ability to run and devise weapons, men needed an array of virtues designed to test and toughen. Obviously, rituals promoting a passage to manhood were associated with hunting and fighting skills. . . .The man was brave, tested against the animals and the elements in almost every hunting society, deliberately separate from the company of women.

Physical courage, the self discipline needed to withstand pain, the patience needed for the hunt—even, one might argue, the quality of silence, which was less important at the hearth—all were taught by example, then probed. One was not born a man. One learned to be a man, acquiring characteristics that exaggerated some natural attributes and repressed others, such as the desire to run from danger. Not all boys could make it. In few later societies could all boys fully become men; in few did all males not worry and wonder, growing up, if they had the potential to do so.

As Stearns informs us, skills and qualities developed for the hunt remain attributes of masculinity even today. Participation and interest in team sports are primarily a male past time; the interpersonal dynamics required for success on the playing field parallel those of the hunting group. Athletes and hunters both must develop trust, provide mutual assistance, and pursue a common goal. Hunting, like sports, was a collective undertaking. Male bonding, a term often uttered with condescension or skepticism, can be traced to the hunting group, where closeness and trust ensured survival and enhanced the chances of a successful hunt. All-male groups, targets of modern feminism, survive today. Their important social purpose of providing an arena for developing male identity and an outlet for focusing male energy apart from women is well documented, but often questioned by those whose fear of male collectives grows out of a misinterpretation of the purposes and essential nature of male bonding. Lionel Tiger (1984: iv), quoted in Desmond Morris, considers male bonding to be one of the fundamental elements of human nature.

Human males operating in groups—talking, planning strategies, devising traps, improving weapons, sharing the spoils—became the most successful phenomenon on earth. In the process, the male grouping became an essential evolutionary element in human nature. The urge to form male "gangs" became deeply ingrained in the human personality. Group loyalties and powerful bonds went beyond mere cultural influences.

Hunting analogies are used to describe male behavior today, millennia after the practice of hunting as the primary male role had vanished. Perhaps only the object of the hunt and the techniques employed have changed. Peter Stearns concludes: "Some part of most modern males would like to be a great hunter, some part seeks to transmute the hunting attributes into actual life in modern society. . . and some part will resent female incursion into realms that have served personal identification" (1990: 23).

Agriculture: Settling Down

Between 10,000 and 8,000 B.C., the global population surged from 3 million people—comparable to the present-day population of Connecticut—to well over 5 million. The development of agriculture ensured a more reliable food supply, and this created a society in which male and female roles were profoundly transformed.

Historians often attribute the innovation of agriculture to women, a feasible theory considering that women were already "settled" in the sense that they remained at the hearth while men were off hunting for game and their male identities. Women fulfilled the gathering function among the hunter-gatherers, and seed collection would have been a natural extension of gathering vegetation for consumption, medicinal purposes, or ceremonial rites.

Agriculture, without which enduring civilizations would not be possible, changed human life in several striking ways. Farming was a more efficient use of land resources. The same land area required to support a single member of a hunting society might now feed a thousand. With agriculture, migration in search of food sources decreased, settlement in a fixed location became possible, and encampments sprouted, then villages.

How was man the hunter to redefine himself in this new society? Manhood became a more diversified concept as civilization took root. The various tasks necessary to maintain an agricultural economy were often divided along gender lines. Physically demanding chores, predictably, were male responsibilities. Other societies retained hunting as a supplementary food source, and the ritual of hunting was preserved. The act of settlement among early agrarian societies provided other distinctly male roles. Construction of more permanent structures required physical strength and likely became primarily a male endeavor. Social groups living in a single location also demanded the transformation of many of the hunter's skills into soldier's skills. Fertile land and water were highly coveted commodities crucial to survival and defense, both on land and at sea, became a critical male responsibility as territory became a vital concern. As civilization spread, the warrior superseded the hunter in many cultures as the paragon of masculinity.

The warrior, foremost among male archetypes, is in many ways a variation of the hunter. He embodies almost all of the same qualities necessary for the successful hunter and has been the epitome of masculinity in many societies not dependent on hunting. The fact that no society of relatively long duration and substantial population has dispensed with the need for defense has ensured the endurance of the warrior as a masculine archetype.

In addition to preparedness for warfare, increasingly complex societies, in order to survive and prevail, needed to structure complex social hierarchies. Mystic leaders, priests, and shaman occupied a high level of the hierarchy and offered suitable male functions, distinct from women's, and carried the unimpeachable divine authority religious leaders have historically claimed. As culture evolved, the goddess became less prevalent with time in the pagan religions. Earliest peoples revered an Earth Mother above all, the female power of nature who granted magical, sustaining gifts. But in the later Greco-Roman mythologies, goddesses were subservient to male sky gods; Zeus and Jupiter were the supreme patriarchs of the mythological realm. By the time Christianity and Judaism dominated the Western hemisphere, the goddess image was all but a relic. Both Judaism and

Christianity profess an omnipotent male deity or "father." Judeo-Christian authority structures are patriarchal in the truest sense. The priestess diminished in time and religious focus shifted from earth to sky. As in the heavens, among earth-bound mortals, male moral authority dominated. The priest or his equivalent fulfilled the social need for a distinctly male role.

But many-layered societies gave birth to a diverse range of expressions of masculinity. Through their Olympic tradition the Greeks made athletic excellence an important determinant of manhood, borrowing from the hunter and warrior traditions by emphasizing physical vigor and immense psychic discipline. Of course, such training also served as preparation for combat. The military obviously played a central role in setting the standards for manhood in classical civilization; battlefield valor was the pinnacle of manhood, often elevating men to godlike status. In Greece and Rome, rational thought, too, flourished as a distinctly male province. The mysticism of earlier eras gave way to scientific inquiry, although science remained mostly an exercise in abstract thinking. The accumulation of knowledge was characterized by a belief in male intellectual superiority. The fundamental concepts of masculinity that dominated classical civilization remained influential throughout the Middle Ages and the Renaissance. "One of the basic assumptions of the classical writings on anatomy and physiology," writes Vern Bullough, (1994: 42) "was that the male was not only different from the female, but superior to her." Bullough concludes that at least one major characteristic of medieval man's masculinity never seems to completely fade regardless of historical era. Although men certainly had more status, in terms of gender behavior they had ever to be on the lookout for threats to their masculinity. Femininity in males was regarded as an illness, and many of the qualities associated with femininity were frowned upon if they appeared in the male (31).

Agriculture and civilization called for the first significant alteration of societies' provision for clear-cut male roles.

Following the fall of the Roman Empire in the fifth century, Christianity and Judaism spread over the Western hemisphere and religion became the single most powerful political and social influence. Even the European monarchs were accountable to the Pope, and their claim to rule was based on divine privilege. Jesus Christ, whether one considers him to be the son of God or merely a historical figure, is perhaps the most widely recognized and enduring model of masculinity the Western world has known. Sam Keen (1991: 103) explains the long standing historical and social significance of the Christ figure.

The image of Jesus on the cross is central to the Christian notion of manhood because it dramatizes the issue of will, a recurring theme in any discussion of manhood. . . . Discussions about manhood in Western culture cannot avoid the figure of Jesus. . . .Every generation discovers a different Jesus—the magical savior, the wonder worker, the mystic, the political rebel, the labor organizer, the capitalist, the communist, the greatest salesman who ever lived, the protofeminist, the ecologist. . . .Without debating the question of the person of Jesus or getting our feet mired in ecclesiastical matters and denominational issues, we may liberate a single insight about manhood that continues to be as revolutionary today as it was millennia ago. . . .The question of Christianity, as well as every religious tradition, puts to men and women yesterday and today: Do I find my fulfillment is asserting my will to power over myself and others, or in surrendering to myself and others in a spirit of empathy and compassion? And if I can only be myself by surrendering, to what, to whom, do I surrender?

The next major upset in the realm of masculinity does not occur until the phenomenon of industrialization, which takes hold in the eighteenth century and attains a dizzying pace in the twentieth. We are in fact still in the throes of the upheaval visited on us by rapidly advancing technology. Industrialization tosses many screws into the social machinery and vastly complicates the critical social task of ensuring distinct male roles. Somewhat paradoxically, the industrialization of the West primarily by men cleared the way for a large-scale women's movement, which further unraveled male identity.

Industrialization

The first years of industrialization created an explosion of traditionally male jobs. Factories were needed to produce merchandise, a subsequent demand for offices in which to conduct business arose, and construction boomed. Transportation, too, was taking off in the late nineteenth century. Ocean-going vessels grew enormous. In the expanding United States, wagons pushed west by the thousands and railroads criss-crossed the countryside in the United States and Europe. Industrial growth increased the number of positions requiring physical labor, and men filled them. Immigrants in search of new lives swarmed to America, and those arriving from abroad helped fashion a new nation, both physically and culturally. Many men who left their homelands for work in America left behind the wives and children who formed their network of emotional support and were a primary source of meaning in their lives. Often assailed with ethnic prejudice, immigrant men also entered an unknown group of male competitors among whom they would have to prove themselves. Women's contributions to the growing nation were of course enormous, but the nature of certain occupations associated with industrializing the country ensured that men still had a corner of society to themselves.

As many time-consuming and tedious jobs became mechanized, there seemed no limit to productivity and efficiency. The company flourished, and the mogul at its helm, the Vanderbilt or the Astor, belonged to the new capitalist aristocracy. Out of the industrial economy branched a new hierarchy. The factory, the shipyard, and the chemical laboratory depended upon the coal mine, the lumbercamp, the quarry, and the farm. Capitalism thrived, but not all people did. Some became rich while many languished in poverty. Men, women, and children were exploited. But men, perhaps collectively and unconsciously aware that their own fantastic progress threatened to make them obsolete, claimed the breadwinner role. No longer would brute strength or rational thinking alone assure manhood. Now a man needed money, and the skill to earn money. But the new male provider paid an awesome price for the illusion of economic control. It was women who experienced the new economy as a blessing. Warren Farrell notes:

The location of a man's work disconnected him from the people he loved, thus depriving his life of meaning. . . .creating little deaths everyday. And if he succeeded in all this, he became a male machine; if he failed, he suffered humiliation. Men's performance—inventing, manufacturing, selling, and distributing—saved women, but no one saved men from the pressure to perform. Men did a better job creating better homes and gardens for their wives than they did creating safer coal mines and construction sites for themselves. Few cared that men died by the thousands clearing paths through mountains to lay roads for cars and tracks for trains that allowed the rest of civilization to be served in a dining car (1986: 50).

In fact, Farrell says, industrialization presented women with an increasing number of options and greater personal freedom.

Industrialization allowed women to be connected with the family and . . .increasingly surrounded with fewer children and more conveniences to handle those children, more control over whether or not to have children, less likelihood of dying in childbirth, and less likelihood of dying from almost all diseases. It was this combination that led to women living almost 50 percent longer in 1990 than in 1920. What we have come to call male power, then, actually produced female power. It literally gave women life. It was an almost all-female club that took the bus from the Industrial Revolution to the Fulfillment Revolution (1993:183).

The most important change brought about by industrialization was the relocation of the workplace outside the home. The time fathers spent with their children, and thus the influence they had on them, was drastically reduced. Boys were beset with the task of forging their masculine identities at a distance from their fathers, and the industrial-age father sought new ways to retain his position in the family as a moral model and authority figure. The growth of materialism in the nineteenth century West reflected the new role of father as bread-winner. He who could provide best for his family was the masculine ideal. Commercial competition was the new outlet for the energies once manifest in the hunter or the warrior. Even today, income and occupational success are the measures of the American man more than any other factor.

The Twentieth Century

Some men have unquestionably found it very difficult to adjust to the decades of modification, and so rely on abuse, irresponsible sexuality, gun fetishes, or other devices to demonstrate that they are men. (Stearns 1990: 229).

The question of what to do with males in a given society, as Margaret Mead observed, is paramount. Never has the search for masculine identity been more confusing in its array of options than at this historical moment.

Defining masculinity amid the cultural complexities of the *fin de siecle* is a challenge for the sociologist. One factor contributing to the present condition of masculinity does seem abundantly clear: The consequences of industrialization have not been resolved or even widely recognized. The continued growth of technology and the feminist movement have added to the pressures on the man searching for a uniquely male meaning. Technological growth disconnected men from the home and undermined their authority there, but for a time work provided a sphere that men could call there own. Tough as it was, the bread-winner role was the male role. The recent decades of change have dismantled even this role. Women have entered en masse many fields once considered the domain of men. The despair of the industrial male persists. Modern events and a changing economy simply tied another loop in the knot of manhood.

Contemporary men express their masculinity in numerous ways, and a handful of masculine "types" seem to prevail. In *American Manhood* (1993), Anthony Rotundo identifies some of the more popular masculine ideals men are playing out in the twentieth century (286-287). The Existential Hero, unable to find an outlet for his masculinity in mainstream contemporary society, lives as an outsider. He is a cynic, casting a suspicious eye on authority, women, and civilization in general. Humphrey Bogart and Ernest Hemingway typify the Existential Hero. The Team Player, writes Rotundo, "struggles to reach the top within his own organization through fierce competition with his teammates, [while] he also cooperates with them in the contest between his organization and others." The Pleasure Seeker, exemplified by Playboy publisher Hugh Hefner, pursues the good life through female beauty and acquisition of material goods. While Rotundo's models define some of the more common manifestations of male energy, the possibilities seem endless and confusing. The lack of a popular consensus about manhood spells trouble for both men and women.

Not only does late twentieth-century masculinity elude definition, but men themselves are under fire. I do not think it an overstatement to call the present search for masculinity a desperate one. Men grappling with their identity frequently find that the very systems of support through which they might attain reassurance have drawn disapproval. The men's movement and any group associated with it is dismissed as a backlash or a fad. Exclusively male groups of various kinds are viewed with disdain. Many recent court cases document a woman's efforts to gain entrance into an exclusively male institution or group. Popular feminism declares a war on violence against women, while attempting to block the channels through which men themselves seek to confront the same problem.

MEN'S SOCIAL ISSUES

For the sex touted as having all the advantages, men display an uncanny level of powerlessness. Almost everyone is familiar with the fact that men die, on average, about eight years earlier than women in the United States, a statistical disparity that exists in all industrialized countries. American males have a suicide rate at least four times that of women, and seven out of every ten alcoholics are male. These are just a few of the statistics that reflect the mental and physical health of our so-called privileged sex. Can we account for them? If we look more closely at the position of men in society—their occupations, family life, up-bringing, and other factors—we can see male power for the myth that it is.

The doctor attending the delivery of a newborn cries, "It's a boy" or "It's a girl." Considering the trauma of childbirth, "It's alive and healthy" seems a more fitting and desirable proclamation at such a critical moment, but sex is important. The difference matters. While the biological forces of sex can never be entirely subverted, social forces compound the work nature has done.

Boys receive less affection than girls from birth onward. The female child receives greater attention to personal needs, has her cries answered more quickly, and is soothed more when ill or injured. The baby boy is spoken to not only less frequently, but less softly than the girl. The fallacy that boys are emotionally tougher than girls prompts parents and teachers to scold or punish them in front of others. Clearly, the sex-specific treatment of babies can have consequences for both boys and girls. We have heard more in recent years about how the typical patterns of parental behavior teach women over dependence, than about how they hinder and wound males.

Adolescence is rarely without grief for males or females. The strange balancing act between childhood and maturity takes place on rocky emotional terrain. The forces at work on boys during puberty are immense. The well of sexual energy in the adolescent boy rivals many of nature's great presentations; it is like a seismic disturbance or a thunderstorm, equally capable of causing joyous excitement and abysmal mental pain. It is no wonder that things go wrong during this stage marked by gut-wrenching, unfocused passion. Automobile insurance rates for sixteen-year-old males are high, as the car becomes an object onto which a boy may transfer his growing need for recognition as a man. Too often, however, the combination of boy and car is deadly. He has been granted adult power under the law, but he has not necessarily learned to handle his powerful impulses. If he has no other stage on which he can experiment with his limits, no healthy challenges to his need for conflict, the teenage boy will find them in recklessness of all sorts. The high number of automobile accidents involving young men is a sad reminder of the need for moral guidance from an emotionally stable adult male, who can teach him how adult men cope with complex emotions. A young man's ability to appropriately express his emotions becomes especially important as he turns to work as a means of personal identification.

Workplace: Refuge or Prison?

Men, in fact, all people, need to be with others like themselves to define themselves. For a few centuries, the workplace provided men with a necessary male world separate from women. Men went to their jobs for the company of other men, and to form a camaraderie not essentially different from the bond of the hunting group or among warriors. But most workplace environments are no longer strictly male domain, and the consequences of such a change are still unclear. What is clear, however, is how the male orientation toward work can be detrimental. Men still seem more susceptible than women to the negative effects of work, even with more and more women performing the same jobs. Aaron Kipnis (1991: 32) enlightens us about the damaging effects of male identity based on work.

The contemporary fast paced workplace, based on the heroic performance model, is becoming the realm of increasingly younger men
and women who are willing to sacrifice the overall quality of their
lives for glory and economic success. Men frequently destroy their
health through obsessive overwork, attempting to provide for their
families. . .even in this age of equality men are still responsible for 75
percent of the financial support for the average American Family.
Also, women have not moved into the traditionally male fields which
are most damaging due to the nature of the work performed and the
work environment. Men are expected to expose their bodies to greater
danger, abuse, and strain. The most dangerous professions are ones
that have been traditionally filled by men and which modern women,
despite their demands for parity, have been reluctant to enter.

It's time we confronted the mythical notion of men's occupational
privilege. Warren Farrell has coined the term "death professions"
to describe the dangerous, dirty, lonely, and often low paying jobs
that have always been performed almost exclusively by men, and
still are today in this purportedly liberated age. While women
have moved from the reception desk to the board room, men have
remained the cab drivers, street sweepers, ditch-diggers, fry
cooks, coal miners—one could compile an endless list of unglam-
orous, sometimes life-threatening positions. Women show no interest in moving into these "non-traditional areas." The more dangerous or unpleasant a job is, the higher the percentage of men
who will be engaged in that field of employment. For every
woman killed in a work-related accident, nine men will lose their
lives. Men are more likely to endure exposure to the elements,
work with or near dangerous machines or poisons, work irregular
hours or at night, work in isolation from other people, or have
jobs that regularly take them far from home. As if to add insult to
injury, we take the products or outcomes of such jobs for granted.
Few of us think of the unsung oil refinery worker whose was
critically burned, as we sit in a warm car at the filling station,
neither do we contemplate the loneliness of the long-distance truck

driver who brought our favorite culinary delights to the gourmet food store.

True job equity is an impossible dream because women will never replace men in the "death professions."

Emotional Poverty and Men's Health

The gap between men's and women's life expectancy has widened steadily since the turn of the last century. Dangerous jobs and the stress induced by fierce competition for more desirable positions is a major culprit. The ways men characteristically deal with stress probably contribute to an even higher death rate.

As they try to cope with the stress brought on by their present condition, and without an established network of social assistance, men suffer higher rates of drug abuse, alcoholism, and suicide, and die about eight years earlier than women on the average.

If we take sheer numbers into account, suicide, alcoholism, AIDS, drug abuse and heart disease are men's issues. In the United States, nine out of ten AIDS cases and more than 75 percent of suicides are men, and yet report after report speaks of special programs of institutionalized support for women. This inequity reveals how little we value men, compared to women. References to the gender disparity in earnings ignore the fact that slightly more women than men are covered by both public and private health insurance.

Depression reportedly afflicts twice as many women as men. This statistic merely reflects the fact that depression is under reported and underdiagnosed in men, while it probably is overdiagnosed in women. Some have tried to explain the supposed higher rate of depression among women as a result of female oppression. Such assumptions do not hold up under fire, however. The reported rates of depression and suicide for African-Americans are significantly lower that the rates for whites of both sexes. If oppression were a factor in depression, African

Americans would certainly have a rate higher than whites, but this is not the case. On the contrary, being in a socially disadvantaged position probably leads to lack of adequate care and underreporting, in which case men, not women, could be called disadvantaged with regard to depression and suicide.

Violence

War may finally end when society begins to hold the security and lives of men to be as sacred as those of women (Kipnis 1991: 31).

War will probably never be eradicated from the earth, but Kipnis raises an important point. Men learn early from a variety of external cues that they are more likely than women to die violently and suddenly, and that they are more likely to be maimed or killed at the discretion of social institutions. Kipnis (1991: 28-29) shares the memory of a man with whom he worked:

Jim recalls a comment from his high-school gym teacher, who reprimanded him for cutting class by saying, "Son, this class is mighty important. This training you get here is gonna give you an edge on them gooks in Vietnam." (28-29)

War is the most obvious example of violence both by and against men. In combat, men become numbers, nameless statistics. Women are certainly not immune to the horrors of war, and millions of women throughout history have been victimized by armed conflict. But far more men have died, often protecting women. Had the 400,000 American men who lost their lives in World War II not made the supreme sacrifice, many American women might have suffered the consequences of an invasion, a terror that is no stranger to women in European countries who perished in aerial bombings or faced mutilation, sexual abuse, and murder at the hands of invading troops. Although women die in wars, it is usually after many men have perished attempting to keep them out of harm's way.

If war is the most obvious and most extreme instance of male violence, then spectator sports are perhaps the most common. Men and women alike spend billions on tickets to watch contact sports like football, which injures thousands of men and high-school-age boys annually. The same is true of stock-car racing and other dangerous recreation, which we accept without question as important leisure activities, even though such events routinely place men in dangerous situations.

Contact crime provides another example of how men are more often the victims of the same violent acts they have a greater propensity than women of committing. Reports about the violence toward women at the hands of men are prevalent. While men do commit most violent crimes, the fact that men are more often the victims of such crimes is seldom noted. Special attention toward violent acts against women illustrate again our women-centered social perspective. All acts of criminal violence are deplorable, but male victims of violence seem less worthy of social attention than female victims. A woman who meets with the terrifying misfortune of being battered or sexually abused has at her disposal a wide range of publicly funded and volunteer support services to attend to her crisis. The female murder victim arouses public outrage and media attention, while the male, unless he was well known or in a position of power, is reduced to a statistic. In 1994, John Wayne Bobbitt became a national joke when his wife severed his penis. It does not take much imagination to realize that a similarly violent act committed against a woman would draw gasps of outrage from a population under the powerful spell of feminist rhetoric.

One frequent oversight in the popular attitude toward women and crime is especially distressing: How many men have risked their lives or their safety to protect women, and how many have lost? We do not usually recognize the male role of protector, only his antithesis, the mugger, the rapist, the murderer.

Men who die protecting women—including law enforcement officers, fire fighters, rescue workers, private citizens, brothers, friends, husbands, fathers—all are unrecognized victims of violence against women. Tonight's news will not acknowledge the sacrifices of such men, but rather will focus on the crisis of violence against women, sketching crude stereotypes of the male perpetrator and the female victim. Recently, in the wake of the O.J. Simpson trial, domestic violence has gained unprecedented public attention. No one seems to question *why* men batter their wives; it is merely stated that they do, and the concluding question always seems to be: "What can we do for the women?" If we asked, instead, "What can we do for the men so that they don't become abusers?" we'd be better able to prevent tragic instances of battery. Unfortunately, the public does not seem ready for attention to men in this manner, because people wrongly suspect that any such attention somehow minimizes the plight of women. It seems likely that many more women will suffer needlessly at the hands of violent men who could not be helped because a society in which feminist ideas dominate the gender dialogue mistook them for privileged.

MEN IN A FEMINIZED SOCIETY

Although the idea runs contrary to the beliefs of the general population, by and large, we live in a feminized society. Human relationships today are based on what women value. The resistance to a men's movement and the mocking of its attempts to access a healthy masculinity for our times reflect a disdain for men. Anti-male sentiment is prevalent, insidious, and far more detrimental than is generally supposed.

Attempts, many of them successful, have been made to degrade men and condemn all things masculine. Such attitudes have certainly been impressed upon an entire generation that struggles against negative images of masculinity, so far with limited success. The man-bashing crusade of the last twenty years has not, paradoxically, been good for women. Feminism seems unable to grasp one simple social truth: When men suffer, women suffer. It is the man who panics from powerlessness and who has been burdened by constant assaults on his self-worth who strikes his wife or child, damages property, drives drunk, loses his job, and disturbs the community. An increasingly violent and unstable world does not reflect the need for more female influence, but quite the opposite. The apparent decline in civility we observe today calls for attention to the needs of the men who are doing the damage to themselves and their families, disrupting our society. It is fatal irony to assume that the prescription for male anger and violence is more feminism; such an approach is to attempt to extinguish a fire with gasoline.

If the women's movement and the sexual revolution were an earthquake, we are in the midst of a powerful aftershock; it is no coincidence that men are beginning to deal with their damaged image just as many women are abandoning the feminist mainstream.

As I close this chapter to proceed with a head-on confrontation of feminism, I offer B. Mark Schoenberg's words (1993: 19), which sum up the current climate for men confronting feminist criticism.

Feminists are wont to believe that men have to accept slings and arrows as part of the penance for the many injustices done to women throughout the ages. It is more likely that men have not reacted because of the age-old belief that men must not fight women. In fact, men have been immobilized because of the historical precedent. Clearly it is time for men to become less complacent.

3

Misreading Masculinity: Men, Women, and Feminism

> By rejecting present society—from political systems to higher education—current feminists have abandoned the fight for equality. By dreaming of an improbable future ruled by age-old notions of femininity, they have refuted the freedom from gender roles. And by promoting their vision, they have closed off every single effective method of activism in the movement. They are, literally, going no place.
>
> Rene Denfeld
> *The New Victorians* (1995:183)

In the following critique of feminism, following Christina Hoff-Sommers' (1994) example, I will differentiate between equity feminism, which encompasses the views of those who believe in economic and political equality between the sexes, and gender feminism, a faction of the politically correct guard who often preach intolerance and attempt censorship and intimidation as a means to gain political and emotional control. The majority of American women probably identify themselves as equity feminists, although the gender feminists enjoy the limelight and attract media attention. Thus, it is the gender feminists who are represented by the term "feminism." As with most political movements, it is the alarmist fringe of feminism that has attracted the most attention, and feminism has subsequently become a monolithic entity in the public eye. Schoenberg (1993: 26) says that:

In terms of stridency, few can match those who preach the gospel of the women's liberation movement. Every community, small as well as large, seems to have a cadre of radical feminists available to seize on any issue that can bring their cause to the attention of the media. Protesting here, haranguing there, the feminist agenda is drafted for maximum visibility.

Having lost sight of attainable goals and increasingly disunited, gender feminism has embraced the bizarre and the fantastic, the scientifically fallacious and the wildly whimsical. Radicals have risen to positions of leadership in the movement and claim to speak on behalf of women everywhere. This trend has continued to the great annoyance and disbelief of sensible women and men who find that contemporary feminists will not accommodate their views. How do gender feminists perceive social reality? John Ellis (1994: 42) described their peculiar slant on sexual politics.

Prominent feminist tell us that men are intent on "destroying, subjugating, or mutilating women" (Marilyn French) or that all heterosexual sex is coercive and hence quasi-rape (Catherine MacKinnon), or that the trouble with men is that they think vertically while women think laterally—where vertical is the (defective) mode of thought that gives us modern science (Peggy MacIntosh). These ideas seem to interest feminists, while the wider public has no difficulty in recognizing their absurdity. Similarly implausible ideas are so pervasive that they can reasonably be said to characterize the present state of the movement; this, in practice, is what feminism now is.

One common example of gender feminist rhetoric is the comparison of the social status of women to the plight of ethnic minorities, African-Americans in particular. William A. Henry, III (1994: 104) provides us with one of the most lucid refutations of this ill-conceived premise:

When blacks point to the cumulative effects of slavery and racial discrimination. . .they are speaking as an identifiable community. Both they themselves and the larger society around them have viewed them as a collective entity. It does not take much imagination to draw a line from the injustices of the past to the inadequacies of the present. . . . Women, by contrast, can claim no such hereditary burden. Their sense of historical grievance is largely irrelevant and almost entirely self-imposed. Whatever happened to women in the past, it is only minimally visited upon women of today. Feminist anger is primarily a theoretical and ideological, not a practical, construct.

The feminist who attempts to equate the tragic oppression of American blacks with the oppression of women commits a double error. Such a comparison misrepresents both the legacy of discrimination against racial minorities and blurs the true nature of the struggle for women's rights.

Modern liberalism, of which feminism is one prevailing ideology, is prone to confuse rights with status. Rights are con-ferred; status must be attained. If particular persons—regardless of their sex, color, or creed—do not attain a particular position in life, this fact does not necessarily imply unfair treatment under the law. No legislative body can ever hope to devise and enforce policy imbuing citizens with talent, perseverance, or drive. Feminist principles tend to motivated by the fight for women's rights. Women today have equal rights; what they do not have in many instances is equal social status. The pre-1920 suffragette had to seek legislative measures to obtain the right to vote. The 1990s feminist, who can cite no law that directly blocks female participation in government or business, confuses rights with status.

Gender feminists are quick to remind their adversaries of the lower social positions of women in the past. History is revised, or at least highlighted, to make women look as oppressed as possible and to make men appear responsible for their unfair treatment. Ellis (1994: 42) offers one reason that the dominant gender feminists are so intent on revising history:

The more the past is or can be made to seem ugly, the more compelling will be the case for change. . . .Reformers are tempted to make
the worst case for the past, in order to convince everyone that change
is needed, but, on the other hand, successful reform requires that the
past be viewed in a sober and accurate way. The rhetorical temptations
of the situation are at odds with its practical needs. In the case of
feminism. . . the rhetorical urge has taken control to such an extent
that the need to disparage the past has completely swamped any
rational understanding of it. The result is so unrealistic a view of what
gave rise to our present situation that it disables the movement.

Feminist-revisionist views of history are most often employed to
justify jobs specially set aside for women. A closer look at women
in the working world reveals a situation more complex than mere
restitution for past oppressions, whether real or imagined.

FEMINISM AND JOB LIBERATION

Many men, and a steadily increasing number of women, have
begun to voice disdain for the woman in an elite job who is
preoccupied with women's oppression. Feminists cite the U.S.
Congress, which is overwhelmingly male, and high-level executive
positions usually held by men, as indications that women still
have a long way to go in achieving rights equal to those of men.

If women have equal rights to pursue the nation's highest level
positions, why, then, do they still occupy a small minority of such
posts? The question is one of motivation and circumstance.
Consider once again the innate sexual energies we discussed in
chapter 1. Men are significantly more likely to be committed to
success in their careers, while a large portion of the female
population will desire children and be willing to adjust their career
goals to raise a family. The desire to raise healthy, well-adjusted
children is at least as admirable a goal as the desire to serve in
public office or in some other influential profession, but the more
outspoken feminists of the last few decades have criticized
traditional marriage as a veritable women's prison. In doing so,

they have suggested that the socially invaluable occupation of child rearing is a drudgery to be avoided. Feminist theory strays into fallacy when it asserts that prejudice is the primary reason women are not proportionately represented in government and other positions of power.

The choice between family and career is so painful that women would rather not make it—and feminist activists are offering the illusory promise that they will not have to. The truth is, however, that in our culture most of the jobs truly worth having, those that are stimulating and demanding and full of intellectual peril, cannot be confined to forty hours a week or anything remotely like it. Working mothers of young children can hardly accommodate themselves to the minimum demands, let alone the maximum and erratically scheduled demands of the best jobs. The ancillary mommy-track is not a dismissal; it merely describes reality. (Henry 1994: 113).

American women are arguably the most free people in the world, more free even than American men. It seems unjust for professional women in the United States, who often earn more than many men, to complain about their oppression. In New York City or Washington, D.C., an Ivy League-educated woman who laments her $35,000-a-year job,—which she performs in a carpeted office with a park view—and finds herself sapped of self-esteem just short of thirty, presumes it is because she is subordinate to the "old boys" who call the shots. In reality it is the often unrealistic expectations, fed by feminist rhetoric, that are responsible for working women's disappointment. Rene Denfeld (1995: 183) is one equity feminist who addresses the supposition that women's failures to succeed in a traditionally male business world can be attributed to patriarchal rule.

Women going about their business today know that things are more complex than feminists paint them. Our workplaces may not be beds of roses, but not necessarily because they're corrupted by evil masculine ideas. No one ever promised us that equality meant paradise. Our culture may sometimes abound with negative images of women, but that doesn't mean there's an insidious backlash being orchestrated against feminism. . . .There is no conspiracy operating behind closed doors. There is only a society of individuals, a society that has changed a great deal in twenty years and can change some more. . . .[P]atriarchal theory only makes sense until you meet the enemy. And then you find that he is just as complex, multifaceted, and often contradictory as you.

FEMINISM AND MEN

It is an article of feminist faith that for woman to become strong, man must become weak. The argument is truly basic to the distorted reasoning that in order for women to gain power, men must be forced to yield (Schoenberg 1993: 26).

Far too many of those who label themselves feminists view men as the enemy. The misunderstandings and distortions of men and masculinity on which feminism operates, along with the reluctance to accept biological and historical realities, are primarily responsible for present upheaval within the feminist movement. The most erroneous supposition is that men share women's sense of sexual security. Few woman can comprehend or appreciate the turbulent journey men must undertake to form and maintain an identity. Being male means an almost constant level of anxiety about where one stands within society and with women. Women, like fish who can't see the water, take their sexual identity for granted. To be born female, in terms of developing a stable sense of self, is to be born sexually advantaged relative to men. Feminism will continue its wayward course until it acknowledges this incontrovertible but widely unrealized fact. As a result of this misreading of masculinity, anything men do that women do not approve of, that makes them uncomfortable or that they simply do not understand is deemed macho or the result of testosterone poisoning. The words "male" and "man" themselves have negative connotations for many. Many feminists overlook the fact that many of the attitudes and behaviors of men, and certain undesirable shifts in society, such as an increase in violence against women, are exacerbated by feminism, but nonetheless are viewed as evidence for more feminism. The uninformed denigration of men and masculinity, which has sustained political movements to undermine male authority and attacked fatherhood, resonates in society. The strife of urban ghettos is partly attributable to the disintegration of a male authority structure. Daniel Amneus (1979: 204-205) explains how feminism inflames rather than reduces violence. He speaks specifically here of the consequences of feminist policies designed to breakdown the nuclear family.

Males have a sexual inferiority complex that makes it necessary for them to find some kind of compensatory meaningful activity which can give them assurance that they are just as important as women. Otherwise they run amok. . . .The ghettos are the obvious example of societies that fail to find ways of utilizing male aggression, and they are kept from capsizing only by the subventions from the male-run society on the outside.

If we can solve the problem of misdirected male aggression, Amneus argues, "There will be fewer divorces; the family and society itself will be stabilized; crime, delinquency, illegitimacy, sexual confusion, and much of the other social pathology associated with the fatherless family will decline" (1979: 205).

Those who believe a world in which women are in control or even entirely equal socially to men would be less violent should heed Amneus' words. Feminism as the cure for violence? Such an approach conjures up eighteenth-century medical practices: Thinking his patient suffers from poisoned blood, the doctor bleeds the dehydrated dysentery victim to death by depriving him of vital fluid and his body's own natural infection-fighting cells. The treatment is seen as unsuccessful, rather than as an accelerant to the patient's demise.

I will sum up this point, that feminism is a self-perpetuating cause, with an idea sure to provoke anyone who even remotely embraces the gender feminist mainstream. A large portion of feminists must revel in the increased incidence of sexual assault against women. The demoralization of men wrought by feminist propaganda has backfired against women in general, but it has fueled an entirely new, larger generation of anti-rape militants. Back to Freedman's (1985: 34) appropriately angry call to arms:

Certainly it is not unfair to say that rape is one issue many feminists hope never goes away. Nothing gets the susceptible more interested in feminism than the fact that feminists are the most vocal in denouncing this barbarism. Sadly, the usual candidate for feminism just does not have the sophistication to see that, besides the rapists themselves, few in our society have done more to foster rape than the feminists.

The attacks on men by certain radical feminists are no less functions of irrational and distorted reasoning than the rapist's resentment of female sexual power, which drives him to commit his brutal crime. Radical feminist writings, almost as a matter of course, contain passages that refer to violent castrations of men, fantasies of male death or intense suffering, and a host of other atrocities that, should they be inverted to reflect similar male feelings toward women, would be condemned at once as misogyny. Freedman (1985: 9) adds:

If Gloria Steinem. . . .had been born a man and had developed the same antipathy for the opposite sex she in actuality possesses now, she/he might well be spending his/her spare hours hiding in the bushes of New York City's Central Park waiting for vulnerable female joggers to come by.

Feminism has become, much to its own detriment, a refuge for the pathological misandryst. There is in effect a socially condoned outlet for the most irrational anti-male rage, the victims of which have little recourse to anything approaching the protection women are entitled to should they find themselves traumatized by a male co-worker who has asked three times for a date. Here we find one of the undying myths of feminism—that sexual abuse of women by men is an extension of men's usually greater social status. In his book, *Why Men Are the Way They Are*, Warren Farrell (1986: 259) suggests another idea.

Lately we have all heard the history of men controlling women's bodies via male opposition to birth control and abortion. But this ignores the turn-of the-century feminists. . . opposing birth control and abortion, it also ignores the fact that the most dedicated right-to-lifers are almost all women who stay away from their families to such an extent that some of their resentful husbands have dubbed themselves right-to-wifers. . . .Rape is said to be an extension of male political power and economic power. If that is so, why do women report black men as rapists five times more often as they do white men? Do blacks suddenly have more political and economic power? Maybe rape does not derive from power, but rather from powerlessness.

It is precisely from feelings of powerlessness that acts of sexual violence arise. Anyone who insists on a safer social environment for his wife, daughter, or sister, should deplore the propaganda and denigration through which feminists knowingly or unknowingly perpetuate the very crimes they say they wish to eradicate.

Violent crimes, including sexual assault, are not perpetrated by males exercising prerogative power over women. Malice toward women does not simply materialize. Misogyny stems from a lack of male self-esteem. Feminists appear to be oblivious to the full scope of social problems wrought by anti-male attitudes. The wife-batterer has already been emotionally defeated when he breaks down and hits his spouse. His violence reflects his experience of powerlessness; he is not exercising some culturally reinforced patriarchal ritual, as feminists like to imagine. A man's perception of powerlessnes today is almost certainly influenced by the constant haranguing and harassment he receives from anti-male attitudes that pervade the media and influence every day interactions. The sources of male frustration that lead to violence go unacknowledged.

Domestic violence is routinely treated as a women's issue. It is
partly the perpetual assertion by feminists that men are evil
merely because they are men that has contributed to some men
doing evil things. It is men who *do not* feel masculine who hit
women.

While more men commit violent acts, violence is not an
inevitable manifestation of masculinity. Much male violence results from a man's being deprived of the opportunity to achieve a
healthy sense of masculinity; feminism too often blocks such opportunities and perpetuates precisely the problems it seeks to
solve. Men as a group are just as anti-violence as women; since
they are more often the victims of crimes, they ought to be. The
victims of current feminist policy, then, are not just men but ultimately women.

If the distorted views of the working world and the family
offered by feminist theorists seem outrageous, their views on the
nature of human sexuality will not be disappointing.

FEMINISM AND SEXUALITY

Pornography reinforces an attitude in men that feminists just don't
like. . . . [C]ensors are seeking to rewrite the psychological and social
rules in every private relationship between men and women. . . .In my
mind they are overstepping their bounds of permissible prescription. . .
Time and again women have confused legitimate grievances such as
harassment and the range of offenses labeled date rape with mere
expressions of opinion they do not happen to share (Henry 1994: 106-
107).

Pornography and rape—according to gender feminists, all of human sexuality in a patriarchal society can be reduced to these two
corruptions. Rape, of course, is among the most hideous of
crimes; perpetrators of such barbarism should incur public dam-
nation and severe punishment. Certain activists, however, have
seen fit to dictate the entire range of human sexual behaviors. A
few, such as Andrea Dworkin, have gone to such ludicrous ex-

tremes as to declare any sex act between a man and a woman an act of rape on the part of the male.

Social research has yet to make any connection between pornography and male sexual miscondust or rape. Gender feminists who sternly resist the idea of women as sex objects fail to comprehend the dynamics of human sexuality. This lack of information directly reflects our current feminine bias of sexuality, which was initiated by the women's movement and perpetuated by men's reluctance to respond in turn. As we will soon see, men who consume pornography, attend strip shows, or engage prostitutes do not feel powerful.

The publication of the *Sports Illustrated* swimsuit issue annually rekindles the debate about the exploitation of women. The blameworthy, as women's groups see it, vary among a market economy, the sexist media, a male-dominated society, or the moral failings of men in general. The fantasy some of these outspoken crusaders would likc us to share is that the models in the photographs were handcuffed, forced aboard an airplane, taken to Mexico against their will, coerced into skimpy swimsuits by bullying photographers and then humiliated by having compromising pictures taken of them which are then published in a high-circulation magazine. I doubt very much that any of the women who pose for the *Sports Illustrated* swimsuit issue would relate their experience quite the same way. Women who win a place in the pages of *Sports Illustrated* stand to make at least a few hundred thousand dollars in modeling contracts and commercial endorsements as a result of their appearances. Other arguments against sexually explicit representations of women confront the unattainable standards of female beauty such magazines promote, and how they breed feelings of inadequacy among women who may not have physical attributes similar to the women depicted in ads and men's magazines. Heterosexual men enjoy looking at attractive women. These images attack men at their most vulnerable point; they could be said to exploit the men whose "oohs" and "ahs" are more an expression of awe than of domination. Women who are aware of their own sexual power over men, and who feel the response to female sexuality have a quite different perspective from those who may feel insecure or threatened by significant elements of their own sexual identity.

LACK OF MALE RESPONSE TO FEMINIST CRITICISM

At this point in my criticism of feminist politics, I suspect there is one looming question: If so many gender-feminist beliefs are ill-conceived or misinformed, why has there not been a strong voice against them? Shouldn't our foremost scholars have been hard at work over the last twenty years challenging feminist distortions of men rather than letting such ideologies plow unchecked through every level of society? They should have. In fact, many attempted it, but did not succeed. As I mentioned at the close of the previous chapter, current attitudes toward men reflect a previously unknown social environment. Men simply have no precedent to go on when it comes to defending themselves. We have been dragged before the court without counsel or even time to prepare a viable case. Another, potentially more disturbing trend has stymied male responses to criticism. The first part of this involves money. Because of its popularity, feminist literature and anything marketable that reflects feminist sentiment is a surefire money-maker. A large, definable market exists for books and other media products specifically related to women's issues. Naturally, publishers and advertisers have to turn profits to survive. The public demands; business supplies.

Economic considerations aside, says C. H. Freedman (1985: 37), "The strange hold feminists exert on the publishing industry extends far beyond the censorship of textbooks." Freedman recounts Dartmouth Professor Jeffrey Hart's story of the difficulty George Gilder endured in the early 1970s as he approached numerous publishers in attempts to have *Sexual Suicide* (1973) reprinted:

Each publisher, seeing a chance to cash in on one of the hottest authors around, greeted the idea with initial enthusiasm; then, a few days later said publishers had had time to calculate the feminist pressures that might be brought to bear against this particular First Amendment exercise—would come a phone call that Hart reported went so: "George, you aren't going to believe this, but we just can't do it."

Fearful of scrutiny that could expose the fallacies behind their movement, gender feminists resort to intimidation and repression. Twenty-three years after *Sexual Suicide* was published, incidences of feminist censorship continue, primarily at institutions of higher education.

Nancy Stumhoffer, an instructor in the [Pennsylvania State University] English Department took offense at a reproduction of the Goya painting "The Naked Maja," which along with reproductions of several other European paintings had hung in her classroom longer than anyone could remember. Ms. Stumhoffer turned to Bonnie Ortiz, a harassment officer at the college. Together they filled formal harassment charges against those responsible for the presence of the painting for creating "a chilling environment." In justifying her action, Ms. Stumhoffer said, "I'm fighting for human rights, for the ability to have a classroom where all my students are comfortable." The liaison committee of the Penn State commission on women found in Ms. Stumhofer's favor: Goya's painting has been removed (Hoff-Sommers 1994: 270-271).

I have intentionally used an incident from academe to introduce a discussion of the area most vulnerable to the excesses of the gender feminists. As we will see, American higher education is under the negative influence of popular and powerful women's studies programs.

OPPRESSION 101: WOMEN'S STUDIES AND THE
TRANSFORMATION OF HIGHER EDUCATION

For the past few years I have reviewed hundreds of syllabi from women's studies courses, attended more feminist conferences than I care to remember, studied the new "feminist pedagogy," reviewed dozens of texts, journals, news letters, and done a lot of late-into-the-night reading of e-mail letters that thousands of "networked" women's studies teachers send to one another. I have taught feminist theory. . . . My experience with academic feminism and my immersion in the ever-growing gender-feminist literature have served to deepen my conviction that the majority of women's studies classes and other classes that teach a "reconceptualized" subject matter, are unscholarly, intolerant of dissent, and full of gimmicks, in other words they are a waste of time (Hoff-Sommers 1994: 90).

Nowhere has feminist fervor been more apparent than on the American campus. The arts and humanities in particular have suffered the slings and arrows of left-wing acrimony. Academic discourse in the arts, literature, history, and social sciences has been sorely tainted by the excesses of feminism and other so-called politically correct causes.

The discipline of women's studies was ostensibly created in response to a perceived need for an academic environment that would afford women the same educational opportunities as men. However, the area became a forum for political anger and personal grievance. Political fashion has been mistaken for scholarship, and, by actively stifling thoughts that do not conform to established beliefs, women's studies are non-progressive and have undoubtedly hampered the intellectual and social development of capable women. Gender feminist figureheads offer their followers little more than dogma and rhetoric, all the while repeating a firm commitment to diversity and equality.

The unfortunate result of women's studies curricula is that such courses do not provide bright and impressionable young women with an opportunity to excel, but rather, as Hoff-Sommers says "They divert the energies of students—especially young women who sorely need to be learning how to live in a world that demands of them applicable talents and skills, not feminist fervor or ideological rectitude" (Hoff-Sommers 1994: 90).

If those who established women's studies set out to prove that women were as capable as men of top-notch scholarship and academic competence, they appear to have made a good case for the opposition.

Women's studies courses are unlike any other course offered on the contemporary American campus. Such courses range in content from reading Virginia Woolf, to rap sessions about the tyranny of the patriarchy, which are nothing short of propaganda in their unfounded attacks on men and the tendency to blame sexism for every hurdle a woman may encounter.

WORD WARS

Linguistic reform is perhaps the most visible indicator of the highly political nature of women's studies. The use of "herstory," as opposed to the phallocentric "history" is a widely known example of politically correct speech. Citing the feminist use of "ovular" instead of the sexist term "seminar," Hoff-Sommers (1994: 50) demonstrates just how far the academic feminists have taken this verbal absurdity: "biological coinages are very much in favor. . . .Feminist literary critics and feminist theologians. . . may refer to their style of interpreting texts as 'gynocriticism' or 'clitoral hermeneutics,' rejecting more traditional approaches as inadmissibly 'phallocentric'." How does the participant in an academic conference, male or female, keep a straight face during a discussion of "clitoral hermeneutics?"

Is the scholarly experience of men and women radically different? Does the fact that a poem, novel, or research produced by a woman make it special solely because of the sex of the writer or scholar? Virginia Woolf is popular among women's studies scholars, in part because she was widely accepted as a prominent literary figure long before women's studies became a driving force in the humanities. Woolf herself denounces the identification of a piece of writing as "women's literature." New York University Professor Carol Iannone (1993: 63) explains Woolf's position:

In "A Room of One's Own". . .Virginia Woolf decides, after some speculation on the specificity of women's writing. . .that "it is fatal for anyone who writes to think of their sex. . . .It is fatal for a woman to lay stress on any grievance; to plead even with justice with any cause; in any way to speak consciously as a woman. And fatal is no figure of speech; for anything written with that conscious bias is doomed to death." It would seem that with these words Woolf could not have distanced herself further from what contemporary literary critics have wrought, often in her name.

As Ianonne's analysis reflects, literary theory seems especially vulnerable to infiltration by gender feminism, but no discipline within the humanities and social sciences has not felt its touch. To the dissenting few who question the validity of gender feminist interpretations of literature and other academic disciplines, it might seem as though the misinformed gender radicals who have infiltrated higher education are unimpeachable. It will probably take half a generation or longer to correct the current trends. Thousands of women are now deeply invested—emotionally, intellectually, and financially—in women's studies. The programs are solidly entrenched into American college curricula. But a movement is afoot that counters the new feminist hegemony. Scholars and writers like Paglia, Hoff-Sommers, and Ianonne give hope for the future. I will sum up with the optimistic conclusion of Hoff-Sommers (1994: 275).

Feminists are only just becoming aware of the fact that the Faludis and the Steinems speak in the name of women *but do not represent them.* . . .Once their ideology becomes unfashionable, many a gender feminist will quietly divest herself of the sex/gender lens through which she now views social reality and join the equity feminist mainstream. I do not think this will happen tomorrow, but I am convinced it will happen. Credos and intellectual fashions come and go but feminism itself—the pure and wholesome article first displayed at Seneca Falls in 1848—is as American as apple pie, and it will stay. (emphasis in the original)

4

Ritual Space: The Mythopoetic Men's Movement

For many, the term "men's movement" conjures up images of Mythopoetic groups whose spiritual work centers on recovering mythological images of masculinity. Masculine archetypes, such as the Warrior, the Hunter, and the Trickster, provide role models of sorts. Highly symbolic and poetic, myths offer an intellectual and spiritual approach to the enigma of masculinity. The images of manhood extracted from these stories are useful in understanding our roots and offer alternate ways of thinking about ourselves as men that do not lead to self-destructive or anti-social behavior. Combining anthropology, psychology, and literature, the Mythopoetics survey the rarely analyzed regions of masculine consciousness, giving central importance to the developmental milestones of boys on the road to becoming men.

Robert Bly is the undisputed pioneer and architect of the Mythopoetic philosophy. The silver-haired poet and story-teller crystallized the men's movement with his *Iron John* in 1990. The best-seller was as fundamental to the loosely bound groups of the men's movement as Friedan's *Feminine Mystique* was to the women's movement more than thirty years ago.

For the Mythopoetics, men's legal rights or social issues are not of primary concern. Any of the social problems typically attributed to men—violence, sexism, anger, or personal unhappiness—are the result of men losing touch with their bonds to nature, or an inner self that reflects a kind of male gender heritage or archetype. According to Robert Bly and his followers, twentieth-century men are, in a way, living a lie. Men were not meant to work at desks or in factories. Human beings of both sexes are complex animals with a strong attachment to nature of which they have been gradually deprived over the course of history. For this reason, the Industrial Revolution and the resulting emotional rift between father and son are of critical importance to the Mythopoet.

Many question practices associated with the movement; certain aspects have a cultist, commercial quality. Few men feel compelled to spend a weekend in the woods smeared with paint, enacting an ancient hunt and reading poetry by the fire and beating a drum. The idea of returning to the wilderness seems valid enough. Separated from the structures of society that support our identities, we are forced to confront a deeper, truer self. We forget our human nature as we become preoccupied with the complexities and artificialities of contemporary life.

If nothing else, Robert Bly can take credit for bringing the issue of masculinity to national attention. Whether one sees the Wildman weekend as a marketing ploy or as an opportunity for personal growth, there is a richness to Bly's work that cannot be overlooked. For those of us comfortable with abstraction and literary allusion, myth reveals a fascinating spectrum of male images that could be internalized and consulted in time of need. Historical images of the ways men lived and became initiated reflect the essence of masculinity and are difficult to locate from a windowless cubicle on the seventeenth floor of a high-rise office building or from behind the wheel of a sports car.

Jungian psychology is a necessary component of the mythopoetic philosophy. Feminists have long used Jungian ideas to explore and explain female psychology, and this strand of the men's movement is following suit. Male ritual initiation also plays a role in the spiritual approach. Gone are the days when pubescent boys underwent elaborate, often traumatic inductions into the realm of adult men. Absence of initiation rites in the contemporary world makes for confused men; confused men are more apt to abuse the environment and women and suffer an inner loneliness.

The Wildman is the primary archetype of the Mythopoetic men's movement, and one that got Bly into trouble with feminists. The name evokes violent images. But Bly draws a distinction between the Wildman and the Savage Man, the latter being the undesirable, threatening character responsible for negative male characteristics. I will discuss the intriguing Wildman more in a moment.

THE LOST ART OF INITIATION

Among primitive cultures, rites of manhood were common. Every people marked in some way the passage from boyhood to manhood. The moment when a boy was welcomed into the world of adult men took many forms. In Africa, for example, the boy of the Kikuyu tribe was taken from his parents by a group of older males who pass around a bowl, into which they let flow a bit of blood from an open vein. When the bowl came to the boy who was to be initiated, he was encouraged to drink, learning in the process that there is a crucial nourishment that he could only receive from other men. He also witnessed the use of a knife for a non-aggressive purpose. The budding tribesman was then able to feel confidence and pride in his membership in the male world. The Kikuyu boy, like adolescent males in many cultures, learned additional spiritual values through songs and legends.

I have discussed the importance of the father in a boy's psychic growth. However, the initiation of which Bly speaks is best left to males other than a boy's father. Too much tension exists between father and son because, Bly quipped to Bill Moyers in a PBS interview, "They're both interested in the same woman." Where are the sacred rituals of initiation in the modern world? Who are the initiators? For boys today, the transition from childhood to manhood seems especially blurred. Bly (1990: 55) says:

> We sometimes assume that contemporary initiation is accomplished by being confirmed, or receiving the Bar Mitzvah ceremony, or getting a driver's license. To receive initiation truly means to expand sideways into the glory of oaks, mountains, glaciers, horses, lions, grasses, waterfalls, deer. We need wilderness and extravagance. Whatever shuts a human being away from the waterfall and the tiger will kill him.

Aaron Kipnis (1991: 169) says that the role of the adult male initiator is to "wound a young man's typical sense of unlimited ability without inducing shame in the process. The young man was acknowledged as a member of the adult male clan—capable and worthy of producing magic, yet still protected by the strength and the guidance of the elders. . .he's told he will fail repeatedly as he tries to master new powers. . .he is encouraged to enter new experiences without risking shame. . . .He's both limited and encouraged at the same time."

Without a sense of belonging and a safe environment in which to experiment with his nascent manhood, the uninitiated male poses a problem for society. Fatherlessness and the lack of initiation rites deprive young men of the same need. Manhood is learned by example only. Womanhood is much more innate. Much of what it means to be a woman is already learned when a girl approaches puberty, but at this crucial stage, a boy's identity training is just beginning. As childhood thinking and behavior diminish, something must take their place, lest a psychic vacuum form in a boy's mind. In his writings and lectures, Bly frequently refers to Alexander Mitscherlich's (1991) idea that demons fill the space that the father doesn't. If healthy ideas about manhood are not introduced to him, a boy will take whatever he can get—a gun, a knife, a car in which to drive recklessly. Perhaps he will use alcohol and other drugs to alleviate the emptiness he feels for want of male guidance. It is important to realize that no boy can initiate himself into manhood, and that boys must be guided by an older male or males who have themselves been successfully initiated. Since masculinity is always learned by trial and error, an initiator provides guidance and a safe environment for the experiments that boys do as they learn to become men.

All boys long to be initiated. There is a certain age, perhaps around eight or nine, when boys often experience an attraction to an older male. It may be a teacher, an older boy in the neighborhood, someone whom the boy has come to trust and admire. He will look to that adult male for cues, emulate him. For the boy to be genuinely initiated, however, the older male must recognize the boy's interest in him and actively show interest in his growth. In ancient Greece, as classics majors are sure to recall, boys established relationships with older men for the purpose of teaching. These bonds became so strong that sexual contact was commonplace, even expected.

DISTRUST OF OLDER MEN

The older man (or the older woman, for that matter) is not currently an object of reverence in Western culture. He is not viewed as an experienced and wise adviser but as out of touch, wielding undeserved power irresponsibly. Distrust of older men reached a peak amid the tension surrounding the war in Vietnam in the 1960s. Young men, instead of having their cries for initiation answered, were sent to the jungles of Southeast Asia to fight for an ambiguous cause, only to return and receive no recognition for their service. Distrust of older men also manifests itself on a wider scale in the suspiciousness many boys develop about their father's dealings during the work day.

The typical family is set up today so that the boy receives, as Bly remarks, his father's temperament but not his teaching. The contemporary boy does not enjoy the opportunity to follow his father into the fields to observe his work and acquire a sense of what he does between sunrise and sunset. Instead, youngsters watch their fathers disappear out the door to an unknown place, where they will perform mysterious tasks. It's no wonder that young boys who want to know what men do, grow suspicious, thinking that if their fathers do not want them to see them work, they must be up to something less than admirable.

Historically, work has most often defined masculinity. As a result, too many fathers, burdened by their own lack of fulfillment, have little choice other than to bark "Get a job," at their sons, without any emotional teaching. Such a pitiable arrangement prevents a father from teaching his son to be a complete person. Both father and son wind up with a narrow sense of identity based on employment, prestige, and earning power.

SOFT MALES

The prevailing definition of masculinity varies with historical conditions, a product of complex interactions between society and the deeper consciousness. While the Mythopoetic condemns the irrationally aggressive male embodied by the Savage Man, he also reserves a good dose of sympathy for the "soft male." The soft male—passive, sensitive, and feminine—reflects women's recent demands of men. Alan Alda, or more precisely, the character he has often played, has become the icon of the soft male. While he retains none of the negative characteristics of the Savage Man, he is an incomplete person who is out of touch with his true identity. Of the soft male, Bly observed in an interview:

They're not interested in harming the earth, or starting wars or working for corporations. There is something favorable toward life in their whole general mood and style of living. But something's wrong. Many of these men are unhappy. There's not much energy in them. They are life-preserving but not exactly life giving. . .[the soft male is] sympathetic to the whole harmony of the universe, yet he himself has no energy to offer (Thompson 1987: 167).

What the soft male lacks is called Zeus Energy (the female equivalent is Kala Energy), what the Greeks called a balanced combination of bodily health, intelligence, equitable authority, and responsible leadership. Many cultures recognized and embraced such masculine power when it was used to serve the greater community, but shunned it when it was abused for personal gain. In our culture, the short supply of Zeus Energy is evident in the media's images of fathers and men in general. From comic strips to sit-coms and advertisements, the male is frequently portrayed as a helpless child who, unable even to read directions on a container, must appeal to his annoyed but selfless wife for relief from the symptoms of the common cold. Male incompetence has provided the premise for more than a few situation comedies. The sensitive man, who seems to be more of a boy than an adult, seems outdated. He is already an object of parody and ridicule in our popular culture. Men didn't like him, and most women weren't too fond of him either. The problem, Bly would argue, was that he had no Zeus Energy. For the most part, men acted the way they thought women wanted them to in order to remain in their favor. They ended up worse off, pleasing no one, especially themselves. The sensitive guy often knows he's not genuine, but he's ill-equipped to establish another more viable image for himself when both men and women break the news to him that he's incomplete.

OF MYTH AND MEN

Myths do not die, they change. In the course of their development they are altered by the shifting beliefs of humanity. . . even if there remains only traces of the civilization which conceived of them. Sometimes, myths even become entangled with each other and their contents overlap. . . .For this reason, it would be better, perhaps, to consult them than try to destroy them (Comte 1991: 14).

Present day attitudes toward mythology underlie much of the

criticism of the Mythopoetic men's movement. In our highly technologized world, myths have come to be regarded as fanciful stories, fictions with no purpose other than to amuse us or explain the social characteristics of primitive peoples. No society, including our own, has survived without myths of some sort. Vanderburg (1985:167) refers to myth as a type of "cultural gyroscope" that keeps a society on course. Myths give the members of a society "the sense that their individual and collective being has a firm foundation." When myths "weaken in any way, some members of a culture may begin to have a sense of being adrift, of having no firm roots. . . .If the myths continue to weaken, a society disintegrates as its symbolic home in reality collapses."

Men are indeed adrift; the absence of viable masculine myths is undoubtedly responsible. A cultural undercurrent of anti-male sentiment has deprived men of forming their own "symbolic home in reality," and society as a whole has been jeopardized.

Myths do not give scientific explanations, but psychological and social explanations and implications. The Mythopoetics do not concern themselves with testosterone, chromosomes, or biological heredity. Instead, they create a system of analogies which can be used as tools to understand the deeper feelings of men and their social manifestations. While the biologists continue to unlock the genetic secrets of sex difference in the laboratory, the Mythopoetics will undertake the equally important task of probing the language and symbolism that reflect male consciousness.

JUNG: ARCHETYPES AND THE COLLECTIVE UNCONSCIOUS

An understanding of Mythopoetic concepts requires basic familiarity with the theories of Swiss psychologist C. G. Jung (1875-1961). Jung argued that men begin their lives as whole, unified entities and that the soul becomes fragmented by Oedipal conflict and pressures of socialization. Psychic stressors relegate the male archetypes, or ideal images of mature masculinity, to the distant corners of the brain. The wounded man's task is to restore the missing wholeness of his psyche by discovering and reintegrating the masculine archetypes into consciousness.

Archetypes imbedded in the human mind correspond to the instinctive drives of animals, such as nesting, migratory, and mating patterns. Archetypal images occupy a psychic layer known as the collective unconscious, which lies deeper even than the unconscious Id, the entity Freud thought responsible for a host of primal impulses. The collective unconscious contains the cummulative history of the human race, and its influences are universal and identical in every individual. The collective unconscious is not the product of learning or experience. The personal unconscious, by contrast, is the repository for repressed or forgotten information that has vanished from consciousness. The collective unconscious has never been a part of consciousness; it simply exists, passed on by heredity. Each of us carries within us an enormous variety of archetypes, that surface according to cultural, social, and personal conditions.

Anima and Animus

Anima is the female side of the psyche; Animus is the male side. At birth a perfect balance exists between these images of the eternal male and female. Self-realization and psycho-spiritual harmony occur when a person accepts the notion that both male and female patterns will inevitably find expression, restoring the unity lost in childhood through the separation from the mother figure and the Oedipal conflict.

Warrior, King, Wildman, Trickster

The Warrior is the quintessential male archetype. His name

implies warfare and violence, but Moore and Gillette (1992: 98-101) explain the true nature of the Warrior.

A man who appropriately accesses the archetypal warrior draws upon enormous resources that enable him to live an empowered life. . . .The warrior is alive, vivid, fairly crackling with energy from the sacred dimension! . . .Hidden rage is transmuted into energized courage. The warrior is an energy source, one that permits us to be assertive about our lives, goals, needs, and causes.

Many of our endeavors call for the personal drive Moore and Gillete describe: finishing a book manuscript by a deadline, exercising, or coming to the aid of a beleaguered friend. Like the archetypal Wildman, the Warrior is not innately violent or destructive. He is "the legitimate expression of controlled aggression."

The King embodies a higher cause to which the Warrior devotes himself. It is a Warrior without a King who is threatening; he may wield his power for his own gain, with disastrous consequences. The kingless Warrior is a mercenary, a rebel without a cause. The King may be an actual king, or an entity or idea, such as democracy, or whatever one believes to be God. The dictator is a Warrior without a King, serving his own ego directly. Such men, who often have brutal childhoods, suffer from a psychic infantilism because they have not properly integrated their archetypes and thus do not know their immense positive power.

Life is not always about the pursuit of serious causes, of course. The Trickster is the archetype who presides over the humorous side of the psyche. The Trickster is known in some form through history and in most cultures, and makes frequent appearances in literature and popular culture. He reminds us of our need to temper seriousness with sarcasm and irony, to let us feel comfortable with occasional mischievousness. Aaron Kipnis (1991: 144-45) clarifies our need for the Trickster.

The trickster may diffuse overheated, polarized arguments. . . .

Through humor we return our confrontations. . .to balance. . . .[The Trickster's] ritualized form of irreverence often contains a lot of ribald humor and satirization of public figures. It helps ensure that the leadership doesn't get too deeply entrenched in the seriousness of its positions.

The Warrior represents power in the name of a cause. The Wildman represents man's eternal bond with nature. To recognize the Wildman is to recognize our inexorable relationship to the elemental realm, our unrefined masculinity. Uncivilized but inherently good, this archetype is not to be confused with his antithesis, the brutal Savage Man. The *Iron John* story, which I will now synopsize, conveys the symbolic interaction of the Wildman and other archetypes.

THE STORY OF *IRON JOHN*

Iron John begins in true fairy-tale style: "Once upon a time." The setting is an imaginary kingdom. Neither time nor place are especially important; it is the characters and their interactions from which the useful images derive.

In the first part of the fable, a hunter whom the King has sent into the woods has failed to return. Suspecting something is amiss, the King sends a search party into the woods to locate the missing hunter. The search party also vanishes. Before long, the King has dispatched his entire band of huntsmen into the forest, only to have them disappear mysteriously. Eventually, no one dares enter the forest.

Years later, a stranger arrives in the kingdom seeking adventure. Disregarding the danger, he ventures into the forest with his dog. Soon the dog detects a scent, which he follows to the edge of a pond. There, the hunter watches helplessly as a massive hand reaches out from beneath the water, seizes the dog, and pulls him under.

Curious rather than hysterical, the hunter returns to the

castle and assembles a crew of men equipped with buckets, and they return to bail the pond dry to discover what lies at the bottom. When the water is drained, mired at the bottom of the pond, covered with body-length reddish brown hair, lies the Wildman, Iron John.

The King imprisons the Wildman in his court, declares opening his cage a capital crime, and gives his Queen the key to the Wildman's cage for safe keeping.

One day while playing, the King's young son drops his cherished golden ball—a Jungian symbol of his childhood unity. It rolls into the Wildman's cage. To retrieve it, the boy steals the key from beneath his mother's pillow. The theft of the key from his mother, a clearly Oedipal allusion, illustrates the young male's need to separate from the mother's power so that he might be initiated into manhood. He opens the cage, injuring his finger in the process, and releases Iron John. Facing certain and severe reprimand for his deed, the King's son runs away with the liberated Wildman into the forest.

The Wildman informs the boy that he will never see his parents again and sets him to work guarding a spring. The boy unintentionally dips the finger he wounded opening the cage into the water and it turns to gold. With this act, the boy has learned that he possesses the power to heal his own wounds. But the Wildman makes the boy promise not to touch the water again, lest he dishonor the spring. When his hair accidentally falls into the water and turns to gold, the Wildman sends the boy off to experience a life of poverty, telling the frightened lad:

You can't stay here any longer because you didn't make it through the trial. Go out into the world now and you will learn what poverty is. I see no evil in your heart, however, and I wish you well, so I'll give you this gift: Whenever you are in trouble, come to the edge of the forest and shout, "Iron John, Iron John!" I'll come to the edge of the forest and help you. My power is great, greater than you believe, and I have gold and silver in abundance (Bly 1990: 253).

The young boy has various adventures and assumes different roles, each representing a different part of the adult male psyche. At one point he becomes a gardener, symbolizing his feminine side. When the kingdom becomes entangled in war, the young man enlists the promised help of the Wildman and becomes a gallant and equitable knight.

Of course, no fairy tale is complete without romance. A princess, whom the boy adores from afar, knows her suitor only as a brave knight and is unaware that he is also the gardener who works for her father. Eventually he reveals his identity to her, a revelation that reunites the female Anima and the male Animus, and the two are married in fairy-tale fashion.

At the close of the story, we witness Iron John as he declares his emancipation from enchantment, thus implying the potential for good in the mysterious and feared power of the Wildman: "I am Iron John, who through enchantment became turned into a Wildman. You have freed me from that enchantment. All the treasure that I own will from now on belong to you" (Bly 1990: 259).

At the bottom of the mind's pond lives a mysterious, hair-covered beast. If neglected, he is a source of fear and danger to the uninitiated. Bly warns us that for generations we have steered clear of him, living in fear and depriving ourselves of the instinctual power of the Wildman. Iron John's confinement to the cage in the story illustrates the fear surrounding him, but also shows how he must be brought out into civilization where men may see him. Rather than suppress him and suffer the destructive consequences, we must accept the Wildman as the ultimate male mentor whose powers for good are latent in the psyche of the uninitiated boy.

THE WILDMAN WEEKEND

Nearly 100 men gathered at the beginning of last summer in a lodge in the Mendocino Redwoods—much as men have gathered for centuries, to sail the sea, to tame the wilds, to play music, to be together. . . .We drummed, told each other stories, ate and drank, recited poetry, sweated, challenged and entertained each other. We were soon outside our regular daily experiences and into "mythological time." (Bliss 1987: 163)

Insulated from women and the influences of civilization—in the Texas hills or deep in the Adirondacks—barefoot, shirtless men, wearing masks of African gods, bathe in the glow of fire light. Therapists and ministers, executives and professors, doctors and dentists constitute the throng of predominantly white, upper-middle-class men. Many have suddenly been struck by the feeling that their lives are incomplete. Fueled by the determination to regain control of their destinies, they begin a soul-stirring descent into grief, facilitated by an initiated elder. In the confinement of a structure crudely fashioned from tarps and trees, and heated sauna-style by a mound of glowing rocks, they re-enact purification rituals in the Native American tradition. Eventually, one brave man comes forward bearing the adorned staff that grants him the right to speak without interruption. He does not relate the highlights of a sports event, as he may have done in the dark of a pub the night before, or engage in political discussion. Instead, with genuine emotion, he laments the wounds of his childhood and the remoteness of his father. Soon he is weeping, joined by other men who tap into the collective sense of grief that comes from modern man's alienation from nature and the breakdown of close contact with his fellow men. Casting fear of public ridicule aside, men who only yesterday competed fiercely with one another in the corporate arena hug one another in an affirming gesture that leads to an uninhibited session of dancing and drumming. The rhythm defines the area within reach of its sound as ritual space.

Such is the image of the men's movement in the mind of the general population. The media were sufficiently intrigued to give the weekend retreat extensive coverage, and the peculiar meetings fast became material for the stand-up act and the sitcom writer.

Bly and his movement have drawn considerable criticism. Certainly there is much to mock if one is unfamiliar with the deeper meanings of the Mythopoetic men's movement. Furthermore, the anti-male media seem unwilling to give the Wildman a fair hearing. Certainly, viable criticisms of Bly's work do exist and deserve consideration.

The most detailed and formidable critique of *Iron John* is *Hammering Hot Iron* (1993), Charles Upton's exhaustive analysis of what he perceives to be a liberal bias in Bly's ideology.

The myths [Bly] presents in *Iron John* are in some ways those of a fading liberalism and an all but dead counter-culture in the process of being transformed into folklore; they are more or less the dominant myths of whatever sectors of society do not identify with the words conservative or fundamentalism. . . .The [Mythopoetic] men's movement is not primarily a movement of ideas, but one of experience and relationships. For this reason, it can't be fully evaluated in terms of the words it generates. . . .The errors in Bly's vision are the unconsidered beliefs of liberal humanism. As conscious values, they are of real worth, but as received ideas, they blindly replicate themselves within our psyches and result in the kind of automatic behavior that destroys the very values on which they are based. (Upton 1993: 221)

However effective Bly has been at consciousness-raising, there does seem to be a gulf between the mythopoetic philosophy and the real transformation of human souls and thus society. Clearly the men's movement is multifaceted; those who re-create rituals, recount myths, drum, and dance in the woods represent one face of a larger entity. It would indeed be to the detriment of men if the men's movement became monolithic in the public eye, and I see this as one of the problems with modern feminism. The Mythopoetics should drum on while other men approach the same issues from as many perspectives as possible.

I think Upton's (1993: 219) general assessment of the

Mythopoetic perspective is accurate and appropriate, and thus I close with his words.

Many if not most of us have extensive dark areas in our psyches where we are very far from knowing what's going on. . . .If this were not true, psychology would be a useless art instead of a limited one. So if the men's movement is contributing to rather than simply filling men with another set of ready-made beliefs, attitudes, self-images, and if it can resist the temptation to masquerade as religion, then it can prepare the psychological ground for real psychological growth.

APPENDIX: MYTHOPOETIC TERMINOLOGY

Anima/Animus: The Anima is the feminine part of the psyche; the Animus is the masculine part of the psyche. Everyone has both Anima and Animus.

Archetype: A model or prototype of behavior passed from generation to generation through the **Collective Unconscious.**

Bly, Robert (b. 1925): American poet; recognized as the father of the Mythopoetic men's movement. Bly's Book, *Iron John* (1990), is foremost in men's movement literature.

Collective Unconscious: The psychic level supposed to contain the cumulative history of the human race. It is identical in all people regardless of historical time or place.

Father Hunger: Phenomenon caused by the Industrial Revolution and the feminization of society, which leaves young males without role models or initiators and thus prone to violence and other unhealthy behavior.

Iron John: Main character of Robert Bly's translation of a Grimm's fairy tale, a personification of the **Wildman.**

Jung, Carl Gustav: (1875-1961) Swiss psychologist whose concepts form the basis of Mythopoetic philosophy.

King: The archetype who represents the higher good or cause to which the **Warrior** dedicates his service.

Ritual Space: An area, usually a natural setting, where men can meet free from the influences of civilization and women.

Soft Male: The over-feminized, falsely sensitive male who acts according to social expectations at the expense of personal fulfillment and complete personal development.

Sweat Lodge: A crude structure made from trees and tarps in which men enact various primitive rituals. The lodge is heated with stones like a sauna.

Talking Stick: An ornate staff, the holder of which is the recognized speaker at certain Mythopoetic men's meetings.

Trickster: A (usually) male archetype common to most cultures in various forms. The Trickster is cunning and deceptive, with a propensity toward humor and whimsical actions.

Warrior: One of the principal male archetypes. Not necessarily a soldier, the Warrior is equitable and ethical in his use of force. The Warrior is often devoted to a greater cause without concern for personal gain. The Warrior acts in service to the **King.**

Wildman: An archetype of the elemental, primitive masculine. Centuries of modernization have imprisoned the Wildman in the collective unconscious from which he seeks to be liberated.

Zeus Energy: Positive, constructive use of male energy for the good of the community or mankind.

5

Manhood in the Mirror: Men, Masculinity, and the Media

THE ROLES OF MEDIA

Feminist critics target media images that portray women in ways they feel are demeaning or unhealthful, citing countless offenses in advertisements and films. Slender, shapely female bodies induce feelings of inadequacy among less-than-perfect women, such critics claim, or the casting of a woman in a part that calls on her to perform menial tasks—and even child rearing can be menial—reflects the oppressive nature of patriarchy.

While stereotypes of women in the media are real, gender feminists, once again, misunderstand the dynamics of sex difference and believe narrowly that only women see themselves stereotyped in ads and TV shows. As we will see, men also are confronted with stereotypes of their sex, demeaning images, and unattainable ideals of male physical appearance, financial success, and athletic prowess.

We must also realize that to some extent, stereotypes are unavoidable. Because the term "stereotype" is such a buzzword, it is worthwhile to examine its communicative function. Stereotypes are especially useful to advertisers and writers of drama and comedy. Dimbleby and Burton (1985:169) remark:

The media use stereotypes of people as a kind of shorthand for getting their message across. It is easier to represent a stereotype than to describe and build a full character. But while the media are guilty of reinforcing stereotypes they have not invented them. They use them because it is known that they are used and understood by society in general. They offer an easy point of contact.

Certainly, as Dimbleby and Burton go on to explain, one is apt to feel uneasy seeing oneself stereotyped. While most of us can laugh at a good mother-in-law joke, a mother-in-law herself may not find such a joke particularly humorous, however clever. Neither do men, or any other definable group, escape feeling tension when they see the collective with which they identify stereotyped. Because stereotypes appear most frequently and recognizably in ads, this is the aspect of media that I will consider first.

Those who protest media portrayals of various groups because of their potential to influence media consumers are correct inasmuch as they recognize the media as driving agents of social and cultural change. The mass media rank among the family, the school, and cultural tradition as forces that shape perception and behavior. The much-studied effects of violence and sexual imagery on various audiences fuel ongoing debates that have become more pronounced during the 1990s.

It is beyond doubt that the media exert influence on human behavior. The exact nature of that influence and the complex interaction between the media and a spectrum of other socializing agents are, at least for the moment, unclear. An in-depth analysis of the media as agents of social change is not possible in these pages. Neither is such a study necessary to consider how men and masculinity are presented by the mass media, and how such messages work their way into our consciousness. One indicator of the media's influence on contemporary culture is their undeniable prevalence. The idea that various media influence our thinking is argued by Greenberg (1980), who describes how the life of the average modern man and woman has been pervaded by media. He determined that the typical American male had roughly five hours of "free time" per day, the time left over after sleep, work, and daily personal care. Of those five hours, Greenberg (1980) calculates that by the mid-1970s

over three hours—on the average—were going to television watching. . . .On top of that radio listening averages some two hours a day. . .a newspaper is delivered to 90 percent of all homes, and some 15 to 30 minutes is spent with the paper. Our typical American also probably looked at some magazine in the last week.

Greenberg suggests that while television ownership rose from the mid-1970s to the mid-1980s, television viewing increased during the same period by one hour per day per adult. Children, with more free time, average more than four hours per day of television watching.

Given their central status in the daily lives of most Americans, how could television, radio, and periodicals not have some effect on feeling and behavior? Advertisements, after all, have been shown to increase sales. While we cannot always establish a simple, direct causal link between the media and society, I think the cliche of the media as a mirror gives a sufficient picture of its power for the purposes of our discussion of gender representation. McQuail (1994: 65) says those who embrace this metaphor perceive the media

as a mirror of events in society and the world, implying a faithful reflection (albeit with inversion and possible distortion of the image), although the angle and direction of the mirror are decided by others, and we are less free to see what we want.

With McQuail's description in mind, let's contemplate how men and manhood are reflected in the media looking-glass.

IMAGES OF MEN AND MASCULINITY IN
ADVERTISING

Crusades against the advertising industry for portraying women in a demeaning light are not uncommon. Many women's organizations and activists have sought to promote awareness of female stereotypes in television and print advertising. The Los Angeles chapter of the National Organization for Women (NOW) annually hands out Turkey Awards to corporations whose advertising members feel to be anti-female. To NOW and similar groups, "anti-female" is a broadly defined term that echoes the assumptions about sex and society that gender feminists typically embrace. A representative anti-female ad might depict a young woman and suggest somehow that she donned a tight sweater to attract men—impossible as such a motivation may seem. Or perhaps a pretty, smiling waitress attends to a well-dressed male customer, illuminating the supposed patriarchal society in which women are subservient to men.

In the early 1990s, a large American beer company came under fire for a television advertisement in which scantily clad models on water skis, dubbed the Swedish Bikini Team, were used to extract dollars from the predominantly male beer-drinking market. Most advertising is inane, and this particular spot was no exception. However, anyone with a reasonable sense of humor (who is not transfixed on the women) could simply roll back his or her eyes and anticipate the next equally silly commercial. But women's groups are not known for humor, and the Swedish Bikini Team became a target for feminist resentment.

Taking their cue from the highly publicized arguments against negative commercial portrayals of women, men too have begun to question the way in which Madison Avenue uses images of men and masculinity to sell everything from socks and pet food to automobiles and package vacations. But men's complaints about what they see as negative or stereotypical reflections of themselves have not been heard, drowned out by the louder din of the better organized and politically powerful women. Men are, incidentally, shown in an unflattering or wholly undignified manner as often as women, if not more often. In 1986, Robert Keith Smith expressed his anger over the public's failure to recognize the many situations in which men are degraded by TV advertising.

Fruit of the Loom commercials portray an elderly lady holding up men's shorts while several men dressed as various fruits surround her. The male sex is made to look as foolish as possible. Or how about the Hanes underwear commercials? One features the invisible Hanes Man, a pair of undershorts and undershirt walking around and being captured by two policemen. Another shows a man in an elevator being stripped by several women. The man stands there, a simple look on his face, and lets it happen to him, encouraging the notion that men would let such a thing happen to them. (Smith 1985: 217-218)

Smith extended his criticisms of TV advertising to regular programs, citing "Saturday Night Live" as one with an inordinate number of degrading quips about male anatomy. Unlike the women behind the Turkey Awards, most male writers who complain as Smith does about the frequency of insulting portrayals of men do not insist on their removal from the airwaves. Rather, they intend to show that both sexes are prone to stereotyping by ad agencies and that men are frequently shown in an undignified or embarrassing fashion. Watch prime-time television for one evening, and you will discover that it is the man —the boyfriend, husband, or father—at whose expense the jokes are made. Feminists who agonize over the so-called sexist images of themselves in magazines and on television seem to have tunnel vision when making their criticisms. I for one always chuckled at the Fruit of the Loom commercials.

COMMON PORTRAYALS OF MEN IN ADVERTISING

Before briefly outlining some of the most common male characters and images in ads, I must emphasize again my stance on gender-stereotyping in advertising. To some degree, gender stereotyping, in commercials and elsewhere, is unavoidable. I would not like to see men's groups imploring networks and corporations to remove ads as much as I would like to see men and media critics acknowledge this fact. While both men and women are shown as stereotypes, at this moment in history, the popular feminists hold the podium. I hope that the following outline will enlighten those who think women are the only ones who are unfavorably portrayed, and provide those who are already aware of this fact with a clearer perception of masculinity as it is interpreted by soft-drink conglomerates and electronics enterprises in the pursuit of profits.

The Ideal Body

The ideal body is what Michelangelo had in mind when he chiseled David from a block of marble. The measurements of his biceps and pectorals seem scientifically calculated and he is always lighted to accent his wash-board abdominals. He sells clothes to men and numerous products to women. He adorns the jackets of the latest romance novels and appears in ads for gym memberships and sports equipment. Sadly, only one in 1000 of us could ever approximate the ideal body.

The Unrealistic Adventurer

The unrealistic adventurer performs highly dangerous work, riveting a steel girder forty floors above the street or bringing down massive trees in a lumber camp—and makes it look both easy and glamorous. The fact that real-life lumbermen in the Pacific Northwest have trouble getting life insurance because of the hazardous nature of their occupations doesn't matter, because when the sun sets, it's "Miller time."

The Super Achiever

The super achiever is a highly respected attorney during the week, and on Saturdays he climbs into the cockpit of his own jet. What time he has left over is spent in the company of throngs of women in cocktail dresses at New York film premieres. Such mythological men appear most often to sell cologne, clothing, luxury automobiles, or products that can easily enhance one's outward appearance or give an impression of financial success.

The Fool or Clown

Many more men than women wear outrageous costumes in ads, such as the Fruit of the Loom Fruits. Men who play the clown might act silly, but sometimes the clown is a true comic character, clever rather than base. The fool forgets to wear his glasses to the beach and trips over a luscious sun goddess who smiles as she asks him to apply lotion to her back. But he hesitates too long, stammering and drooling. When he comes to his senses, she's gone.

The Father

A few ads show fathers as considerate and responsible, as men who are deeply in love with their spouses and dedicated to the well-being of their children. Many more portray him as the loose screw in an otherwise happy and healthy family: "Dad rammed the car into the fence again; good thing there's such and such auto-body repair shop." Or perhaps Mom, busy with her career as an international finance adviser, goes on a business trip and the household falls apart because father doesn't know how to wash dishes or do laundry. She'll need the color-safe bleaching action of Tide when she returns from Amsterdam and rolls back her eyes and sighs at her dependent family. Marketers of cold medicines and headache remedies seem to have a certain affinity for ad copy that describes an ailing husband who can't seem to master cough syrup and who must appeal to his wife for help reading the dosage on the box.

The Criminal or Ne'er-Do-Well

Male thieves, drug users, and street people harass and victimize women in reality and in commercials. The fact that the majority of crimes are committed by men cannot be disputed, and ads showing men who are less than respectable treating women badly or threatening them reflect reality to a point. Scenarios with male criminals and female victims often play on the understandable fears of women. A large poster ad in a Manhattan drug store shows a mugger clutching at a woman's purse. The woman is retaliating with a burst of pepper spray from an aerosol dispenser. The copy below the drawing implies that women are not safe anywhere and that they should carry pepper spray as a weapon against potential attackers. Nowhere on the poster does it say that such a concoction may become tempting in a marital conflict, provided a child or a pet does not discover it first.

Typical Advertising Scenarios

- The woman must explain something to the man that he cannot understand.

- The woman outsmarts or outdoes the man, usually at typically masculine endeavors, like sports, driving, or business.

- Families function in spite of men; mother knows best.

- Men are indestructible, emotionally and physically, and as a result, enjoy "access" to the world's most attractive models, or alternately, they are incompetent beyond belief and some poor woman is left to clean up the mess.

- Men are patently selfish or morally compromising in their pursuit of sex or are sycophantically accommodating to women's demands of them.

IMAGES OF MASCULINITY IN LITERATURE

While studies of gender roles in classical and modern literary fiction and drama are not new, the vast majority of such studies have focused on the roles of women and the way in which they reflect history or the psyche of the (usually male) author, poet, or playwright. With the advent of men's studies, scholars have sought to uncover themes of masculinity in literature with similar intentions. Many excellent analyses of masculinity in fiction have been published, and the list continues to grow. But to clarify the approach of scholars exploring masculine reflections in fiction and to illustrate common themes, I would like to turn briefly to what is perhaps the best-known work in the English language.

Shakespeare's Hamlet is the quintessential male protagonist. A character whose struggle with masculine identity is great, Hamlet confronts the profound and terrifying questions of existence through decidedly male eyes. David Rosen (1993: 62-63) asserts that

Hamlet experiences anxiety both because of the dysfunction of previous masculine roles and because of his shame at their loss, a loss he holds himself accountable for. In this vulnerable situation, without a male guide, Hamlet sees himself as charged with creating a new masculinity. In part he finds his task is to resurrect his father and reestablish the lost masculine powers of his father. On the battlements

of Elsinore, a symbol of masculine ideals. . . Hamlet begins. Danger
surrounds Hamlet's castle. But inside too, unseen pitfalls make the
castle insecure. . . .The opening words question identity: "Who's
there?" And the threat of instability no longer comes exclusively from
without, but from the intimate within.

This double threat, the clash between external ideals and innate
identity, Rosen concludes, is the problem for men of Hamlet's
time. In fact, it is a problem for men of all times. Only the ideals
differ from one historical era to the next.

Hamlet is one man's quest for male identity according to the
ideals of his age. What Rosen calls "the shift from abstract
passion to tangible flesh" describes the male predicament
stemming from external anatomy, which we explored in chapter 2.
Hamlet's struggles transcend historical eras. The nagging paternal
conflict Rosen describes convinces us that Shakespeare's vision of
the role of the father anticipated Robert Bly's Father Hunger by
nearly four centuries.

POP CULTURE MANHOOD

Several specific media deserve attention for their apparent
capacity to convey notions of masculinity. First, comic books, an
American pop culture staple, have been the refuge of many an
adolescent boy traveling the rough terrain of emergent manhood.
Hence such books brightly reflect the essential elements necessary
to an understanding of male consciousness. Film and television
also are significant cultural gauges of important aspects of
maleness. For the purpose of this discussion, I will combine film
and television, realizing that in a more detailed analysis of media,
a distinction would be drawn. I will discuss film with the
assumption that much of what holds true for film in terms of
representations of gender also hold true for television.

For the baby boomers and their parents, television was a still
nascent medium, and comic books were a pop culture standard.
The super-hero comics were consumed primarily by pre-

adolescent boys and reflect a unique set of masculine ideals. Peter Middleton examines the comic book depiction of the super-hero as it relates to such ideals. On the uniqueness of the comic-book format, Middleton (1992: 23) notes:

Film, television, and comics provide armatures on which boys can wind all kinds of fantasy. Comics, relatively low budget, highly targeted and visually simple, offer a useful means of analyzing the pre-emptive structures of fantasy. . . found in most boyhood rituals of entry into manhood.

Middleton expresses his belief that comics or film cartoons serve an important function for prepubescent males because this is a time, preceding full sexual awakening, when resentment of exclusion from the adult male world is a dominant frustration. Comic books and cartoon adventures offer images of hyper masculinity: musclebound soldiers draped in bullets and toting machine guns, or superhuman heroes combining hypermasculinity with mythology. Superman is himself the epitome of hypermasculinity. He possesses absolute emotional control and has no match for his physical might. His only vulnerability (if he did not have one, there could be no dramatic action) is the fictitious element Kryptonite, the debris of his destroyed home world.

MEN IN CONTEMPORARY FILMS

Hollywood knows well that men cannot live by the models of masculinity it proffers. . . . Such heroic images afford men and women vicarious release while rendering them small and timid by comparison. They wish they could know such men; they have no illusions about resembling them. An abiding malaise results in the male, victimized by this comparison between himself and the physical splendor of the hero with whom he has so passionately identified. (Mellen 1977:3)

Who among us has not gone to a film and fantasized about becoming the hero or inheriting some of his traits? Most men can understand why a woman may feel inadequate watching images of genetically gifted women flaunting their perfect bodies on the screen with every heterosexual man's eyes transfixed on her image. Few women seem to understand the degree to which men can find media images disturbing reminders of their own limitations. Many of the depictions of men I outlined in the preceding discussion of advertising hold true for films. One notable exception seems to be the recurring theme of violence in films, which has direct ties to masculinity. Any analysis of masculinity in film would not be complete without questioning the inexorable relationship between male characters and screen violence. The greater male propensity to committing acts of violence is irrefutable, and the fact that movies in the last two decades have grown increasingly violent to the point of becoming a heated political issue is as much a media question as it is a masculinity question. At the risk of sounding redundant, I must reiterate that the purpose here is not to debate a chicken-and-egg problem of violent media and violent society, but rather to view how films reflect the issues of masculinity we have discussed. The details of exactly how the media reflects society, such as how the media arts are subject to supply and demand in a market economy, would lead us away from the topic at hand: masculinity as it appears through the modern media looking-glass.

Much cinematic violence is a dramatic device employed to show the rites of passage of young boys determined to become men. Numerous violent films present as their protagonist males on the way to manhood. Violence, if we stretch the definition to include emotional trauma, potentially scarring fear, or even violent internal dilemmas, seems to be a prerequisite to achieving manhood. In a modern world, where rituals are forgotten, films provide a vicarious initiation experience. As Ben Greenstein (1994: 39) has written:

[Filmmakers] know that boys cannot dip their spears into the blood of a slain lion, so they provide the experience on celluloid instead. Hollywood is now the high priest of puberty, the circumcisor. . . .

Films such as *Top Gun, The Young Ones, Robin Hood, The Magnificent Seven,* and thousands more are as popular today as was *The Wild Ones* when it first came out. As long as boys and men remain what they are, these films and films like them will continue to enthrall. By watching them, a boy can experience, albeit vicariously, his trial by fire, his mutilation, his feat of heroism and his successful seduction of women. It is no wonder these films are run-away winners. It could be argued that the moguls of American cinema are unconsciously perpetuating what their maleness dictates. They are consciously carrying on the functions of the elders of the tribe, the wise men who know instinctively what is needed for the tribe to survive. . . .It is celluloid circumcision.

Instances of film violence, at least those that depict men as the perpetrators of violence, are often employed to show the success or failure of masculinity. The hero, when he resorts to violence, does so as a means to an end, while the villain or ne'er-do-well resorts to violence out of desperation; his search for male identity has been shorted out. Wanton destruction and selfish cruelty are the only expressions of a frustrated search for meaning and identity. Clint Eastwood's *Dirty Harry* movies of the 1970's reveal this cinematic use of violence. Harry Callahan is a vigilante cop, enraged by the criminal element on the street and the red tape in the police force. Out of desperation, he takes matters into his own hands. He becomes a hero by using his power to clean up the streets of Los Angeles, even if it means disobeying his superior officers. We could also say that some of the criminals Harry takes down suffer from economic desperation and an inability to express their masculinity through socially acceptable channels. Instead they choose crime, or crime chooses them. The dramatic action of *Dirty Harry* and similar films is extracted from male desperation, which in reality as well as in films, often leads to violence.

THE NEW AGE SENSITIVE MAN
(AND HIS GUN-TOTING WIFE)

Violence will never disappear from American movie screens, but the association of violence with masculinity—in fact the nature of movie masculinity in general—has undergone a transformation. Susan Jeffords (1993:197) relates what happened to men in movies during the first half of the 1990s.

1991 was the year of the transformed man. There's hardly a mainstream Hollywood film from that year with a significant male role that does not in some ways reinforce an image that the hard fighting, weapon-wielding, independent, muscular, and heroic men of the eighties. . .have disappeared and are being replaced by the more sensitive, loving nurturing, protective family men of the nineties. . .a changed image of U.S. masculinity is being presented, an image that suggests that the hard-bodied male action heroes of the eighties have given way to a "kinder, gentler" U.S. manhood, one that is sensitive, generous, caring, and perhaps most importantly, capable of change.

Perhaps John Wayne is turning over in his grave, but Jeffords calls attention to an interesting turn in American filmmaking that I believe provides further evidence of a feminized society. Women's ideals dictate right and wrong thoughts and behaviors. There is a revenge theme running through today's films, of which 1991's *Thelma and Louise* is the most notable example. As with advertisements, films today are not complete unless a man is outdone by a woman, whether this is accomplished in a simple game of chess, a diplomatic mission, or an ultimately fatal gun duel. Jeffords (1993:198) concludes "There's no one crashing through the doors in 1991. Instead, many nineties Hollywood men get doors slammed in their faces, or they are forced to stand patiently while the women inside decide whether to see them or not."

Mid-way through the last decade of the century, two media manifestations of masculinity seem to predominate: the violent hero reminiscent of Rambo and recycled numerous times by

Arnold Schwarzenegger, and the feminized man, who sits quietly while women show him up. Seemingly in opposition to one another, perhaps these two character types reflect the conflict in every modern male. The struggle between the inner emotion of the feminized male and the outward action of the hero is our version of Hamlet's struggle.

As the twenty-first century dawns, with the inevitable shift in predominant social ideas about gender roles, we can expect reflections of manhood in the media to change correspondingly. Who, we might ask, will be the twenty-first-century masculine hero?

6

Trial and Error: Men, Politics, and the Law

This chapter attempts to illustrate a bias against men in the legal system. On several specific issues, men are not afforded the benefit of the doubt when they stand accused of a number of serious crimes. Husband battery, divorce and child custody, sexual harassment, and false accusations of child abuse signal trouble for men who seek legal recourse and a fair hearing. Tragic instances do occur, but present political fashions favoring women leave the door open for widespread abuse of laws and policies designed to protect women and children.

VIOLENCE AGAINST MEN

Research has shown that violence or threats of violence by women directed at men are more common than is popularly assumed. David Thomas believes that "the existence and status of the male victim has to be acknowledged. In public, the subject of female violence is still taboo." An Englishman, Thomas describes a visit to the United States in which he engaged in conversations with Americans about the subject of female aggression against men. He was astonished by just how many men had been attacked by their wives. One man, a professional photographer, told

Thomas that he had endured ten years of assaults by his former wife before winning custody of his two daughters. Another woman revealed that her partner had divorced his former wife because of her violent behavior toward him.

According to Warren Farrell, police reports from various American cities reflect a ratio of wife battery to husband battery ranging from 102 to one, to two to one. Citing independent social research, however, Farrell says that the ratio is actually one to one: About 12 percent of husbands had inflicted violence on their wives, and about 12 percent of women had inflicted violence on their husbands. Farrell also states that slightly more wives than husbands threaten their spouses with weapons, though men are slightly more likely to use a knife or gun against their wives. Women are more likely to throw objects, while acts of hitting and slapping were committed equally by men and women.

The prevalence of women's violence against men is only one half of the unfortunate truth. Thomas goes on to describe how the law treats men who are victimized by their wives. When he visited the United States, Thomas interviewed a man whose former girlfriend had repeatedly assaulted him, and then called the police and accused him of abusing her. The police would not believe that the man had been victimized by his girlfriend. He would lock his hands behind his back, refusing to retaliate while she pounded him with her fists and scratched him with her nails.

Assault laws do not discriminate against men in the way they are written, but enforcement of these laws in cases of women who abuse their male partners is certainly lacking. A man who has been physically assaulted by a woman has little recourse under the law, not because of the laws themselves, but because of the greater willingness on the part of authorities to believe women over men. Even though he is probably far larger and stronger than his wife or girlfriend, a man cannot retaliate, lest he be deemed the aggressor. "She started it" is not an admissible plea.

It seems that women and men both assault each other, but only men are blamed.

FALSE ALLEGATIONS OF RAPE AND CHILD ABUSE

Increasingly, counselors on sexual issues are not employed to provide balanced judgements or advice. They are there to act upon allegations of bad behavior by men against women. (Thomas 1992: 153)

Aaron Kipnis recalls the experience of a man he knew to be an outstanding father by anyone's measure who was reported to local authorities for child abuse by his former wife after he inadvertently touched his six-month-old son's scrotum while changing his diapers in her presence. When the wife complained to the police, an arrest warrant was issued immediately. No investigating of any kind was done. The man underwent involuntary psychological screening and costly and embarrassing legal proceedings. Kipnis wondered how unlikely it would be for women to undergo such a personal and public trial with only a phone call to substantiate the accuser's claims. The ultimate tragedy of situations like these, which seem to be widespread enough for extreme concern among parents, men, and the legal system, is that men who cannot afford to defend themselves financially or emotionally sacrifice their valuable relationships with their children. I conclude with Kipnis' words (1991: 51), which reveal the most dangerous and frightening aspect of the case.

In this particular divorce, the mother later acknowledged that such a tactic was encouraged by a woman's support group. She was disturbed that the father wanted to be involved with the child because she didn't want him in her life any more.

SEXUAL HARASSMENT

The war between the sexes has taken a uniquely virulent form in today's culture. False allegations of harassment and date rape are springing up like condoms in springtime. Face the facts, men. You live in a high-risk social environment. If a woman brings false sexual charges against you, no matter how flimsy her evidence or belated her action, your protest of innocence may not be believed. This is the time of the Werewolf Hunt. And the last time I checked you looked a lot more like the Werewolf than she does (Baber: 1992: 156).

The main reason that sexual harassment has become a seemingly unresolvable issue is the existence of a social environment whichdoes not encourage women to recognize and take responsibility for their own sexuality. The focus continues to be on male behavior, which, as Baber says, is deemed appropriate only when women give their OK. Feminist rhetoric has shaped workplace conduct codes, and thus the male perspective has been summarily dismissed. Paradoxically, those who exaggerate the incidence and degree of sexual harassment in the workplace do a great injustice to those women who have indeed suffered abuse and humiliation at the hands of male co-workers. Incidents of misconduct do occur, but existing definitions of sexual harassment are too ambiguous and allow for wide-spread abuse.

Many women have been falsely led to believe that any frustration or uncomfortable communication they experience at work is the result of a male environment that, because of its "maleness," is naturally hostile to women. While this notion harms through false allegations and misguided criticisms, it also hurts women who may fail to see the true causes of their workplace problems and prevents them from adequately resolving them.

Sexual harassment is perhaps the most controversial political issue stemming from the recent escalation of the gender conflict. Vaguely defined terms, miscommunication, administrative confusion, and naivete about sexual dynamics have created a monster in the workplace that has been as detrimental to women as it has been to men. False accusations, whether they merely tarnish the reputations of respectable, hard-working men or severely damage their careers, are an obvious problem. But far more frequently, sex-harassment hype destroys the work environment, sacrificing productivity and greatly reducing the fulfillment and satisfaction dedicated professionals of both sexes can gain from their accomplishments at work.

So far-reaching is the arm of feminism as to make the most subtle and superficial interaction between heterosexual men and women highly political acts. On a humorous but nonetheless angry note, Asa Baber has envisioned what he calls the 1990's safe dating kit and suggests a number of measures, including attorney contracts between dating partners and satellite surveillance. Such precautions are indeed outlandish, but so are some of the actual allegations and cases to which he refers. In one Orwellian example, Baber describes a male acquaintance who lectures part time at a public college. This teacher took a female former student, who Baber describes as "bright but insecure," to lunch at her request. The women confided in her former teacher that she believes she is not attractive to men. He responds to her, saying, "You are a very attractive woman. If I were in your age group and single, I would probably ask you for a date." Baber's description (1992: 159) of the outcome of the man's innocent attempts to be compassionate is becoming more and more the nightmare of many a male college teacher.

She goes back to the department chairman, reports that the man has sexually harassed her and insists that his contract not be renewed because he is a threat to women students. The chairman agrees and it is done. The man is dropped from the faculty, no questions asked.

DIVORCE AND CHILD CUSTODY

Robert Bly (1990) points out how the modern father, home only in the evening, receives his father's temperament but not his teaching. There is a paternal absence even in families where both parents live together with the children. But what about when the parents separate, and contact between fathers and their children becomes nonexistent or complicated by custody arrangements?

Before we consider the possible effects on paternal absence as a result of divorce on children, it is worthwhile to explore the father's own experience. A study of 783 divorces by the Austin chapter of Texas Fathers for Equal Rights (See Baumli, 169) in the mid-1980s showed that fewer than one in five fathers who obtained custody of their children received an award of child support, while nearly 97 percent of mothers who were granted custody received child support from their former husbands. Of course, one could argue that in most cases, fathers are earning significantly more than their wives, making the need for child support from the wife unreasonable. But the fact that the Texas study showed that most men who were initially awarded custody lost it within two years reflects the unfortunate condition of the breadwinner. In order to keep ahead financially, most single parents will have trouble balancing full-time work with child-raising responsibilities. In the long run, most fathers end up without legal custody of their children and the burden of providing for them financially, while the wife can enjoy time with her children with reduced financial strain.

The Texas study discovered one other aggravating fact. A look at compliance statistics in child-support arrangements revealed more women to be in default of the agreement. After a three-year separation, seven times as many men than women were in full compliance with divorce decree orders; only 11.7 percent of women ordered to do so were paying.

Political effort focusing on the family must reassert men's bonds with the family and reverse the "lost father" syndrome. While any long-term plan for men's liberation requires changes in the structure of our work and economic institutions, a number of intermediate steps are possible. Other political goals of the men's rights activists include changes in work structure to better accommodate men and women. Flexible hours and home based work might prove to be solutions to men who seek to fulfill a dual role of economic provider for their families as well as remain an integral part of the relationship dynamics, assuming for a moment that a father has deservedly won custody of his children and that the financial circumstances are settled. One man who won custody of his three daughters described the change in his social life as a result of his divorce arrangements:

The fact that I fought for and won custody of three small children [girls], and that I am a militant father's rights and children's rights activist are a definite turn-off to the vast majority of women. My social life has been less than stellar. . . .When it is learned that I have custody of three girls, it is much akin to having contagious leprosy. When I enter the room the women move to the far corner. I think the fact that I am so involved with the men's movement has a great deal to do with it. The first reaction to me at these events is a great deal of female attention, but then when the women learn I have custody, they attempt to persuade me to "give up the girls who need a mother." When I say I think they already have the best mommy any kid could want, ME!, they run and the word gets out (Pangborn 1985: 171).

I conclude by offering a few suggestions that could make the home and work environment safe for women and children without compromising the legal rights of men. Both government and private institutions should set standards for sexual harassment that are more definitive. It is often the ambiguity of the language in these policies that allows for miscommunication and abuse. Husbands should have access to some sort of support system that at the very least allows them to voice their complaints about abusive wives without fear of ridicule. Finally, women's groups must understand the dangers in treating men with disdain through the law; that such treatment will jeopardize the rights of those with legitimate cases. Divorce proceedings should make an effort to weigh equally the cases of husbands and wives and consider men's emotional attachments to children they have raised in addition to financial issues.

Legal bias is an unfortunate reality for men. At this point I would like to shift to consider men's individual roles and relationships, with special emphasis on the emotions associated with them.

7

Individual Men: Life, Work, and Relationships

Until now, this inquiry into masculinity and men has focused on abstract theories of biology, history, politics, and mythology. In this final chapter I will more closely examine the practical side of being male, the everyday considerations of sex difference from a male perspective. Communication, commitment, marriage, infidelity, sexuality, romance—these are issues about which both men and women are immediately concerned. What follows is an attempt to clarify the male perspective on each of a number of issues. Perhaps these explanations will help men better understand their relationships, and help women see more clearly the underlying motives of male attitudes and behaviors.

MEN AND WOMEN

In his colorful *Book of Guys,* Garrison Keillor (1993: 12-14) articulates the predicament of the emerging man in the throes of adolescence. He tempers painful reality with sharp wit:

Girls had it better from the beginning, don't kid yourself. They were allowed to play in the house where the books were and the adults, and boys were sent out like livestock. . . .Adolescence hits boys harder than it does girls. Girls bleed a little and their breast pop out, big deal, but adolescence lands on a guy with both feet, a bad hormone experience. You are crazed with madness. Your body is engulfed by chemicals of rage and despair, you pound, you shriek, you batter your head against the trees. You come away wounded, feeling that life is unknowable, can never be understood, only endured and sometimes cheated. . . .We carry adolescence in our bodies all our lives. . . .Men adore women. Our mothers taught us to. Women do not adore men; women are amused by men, we are a source of chuckles.

Keillor is known for his tongue-in-cheek style, but I think his words relate a truth that many recognize but few openly acknowledge or completely understand. The behaviors of adolescent males are scorned and questioned, but rarely are the particular hardships of becoming an adult male examined at length. The frustrated father or mother chooses to believe that "boys will be boys" and let nature take its course. The trauma Keillor describes stems from the realization in the early teens that manhood, unlike boyhood, will require constant testing and retesting. The male's identity formation will forever depend on his ability to show others—through work, physical strength, suppression of fear, or other accomplishment—that he is indeed a man.

THE COMMITMENT QUESTION

Men are notorious for their flight from commitment in monogamous relationships. Where is the male fear of commitment rooted? What does a man stand to lose if he commits to a woman?

An overriding fantasy that stands in the way of male commitment is the pursuit of multiple women. To marry would mean giving up this fantasy. Paradoxically, women seem motivated by the opposite fantasy: to settle down with one specific man. The male quest-fantasy of an endless string of partners has become more viable in recent history. In *The Moral Animal,* Robert Wright (1994:133) explains how rapid social changes of the last century facilitate the male quest-fantasy:

Since Darwin's day, the incentive structure surrounding marriage has been transformed—indeed, inverted. Back then, men had several good resaons to get married (sex, love, and societal pressure) and a good reason to stay married (they had no choice). Today an unmarried man can get sex, with or without love, regularly and respectably. And if for some reason he does stumble into matrimony, there's no cause for alarm; when the thrill is gone, he can just move out of the house and resume an active sex life without raising local eyebrows. The ensuing divorce is fairly simple.

Although the male propensity to pursue numerous partners is consistent throughout history and is transcultural, Wright reveals why this particular moment in history is an especially difficult one in terms of men's and women's expectations of one another regarding physically intimate relationships. As Keillor (1993:14) puts it somewhat less academically: "A monogamous man is like a bear riding a bicycle: he can be trained to do it but he would rather be in the woods, doing what bears do."

Why do men, generally speaking, treat sex so casually and pursue it with such obsessiveness? As I discussed in Chapter 1, sexual activity for men is an affirmation of sexual identity as it is not for women. Women are aware, consciously and unconsciously, of their sexual superiority residing in their potential to foster new human life. Women can rest assured knowing that they are indispensable to the perpetuation of the species. Men, on the other hand, have a transitory role in reproduction. Artificial insemination makes even a man's physical presence unnecessary to create offspring.

Paglia (1991:19-20) explains men's more ardent pursuit of carnal experience:

Sex is metaphysical for men, as it is not for women. Women have no problem to solve by sex. . . .In human beings sexual concentration is the male's instrument for gathering together and forcibly fixing the. . . emotion and energy that I identify with women and nature.

Social and cultural pressures on men reinforce to some extent the tendency to ardently pursue sexual relationships. A male's sexual exploits are admired by other men and thus serve as proof of one's masculinity among other men. Men do not "lose" their virginity in the sense that women do, so much as they gain evidence, through sexual experience, of their male potency. Obviously, an unbroken string of sexual conquests does not ensure the development of emotional maturity and moral respon- sibility that is a prerequisite to the most stable and productive expressions of masculinity, and sexual union represents only one level of human interaction. As we will now see, it is not the only level at which the distinction between the sexes is remarkably evident.

MEN AND SOCIAL INTERACTION

Women often seem amazed at how long the typical men can go without human contact, and indeed, men more often than women view interactions of substance or quality with other people as unnecessary or even intrusive. Herb Goldberg (1976:44) gives a stereotypical picture of the stark emotional life led by a sizable portion of single American men.

The behavior of many contemporary men is in some ways analogous to the behavior of autistic children. The autistic child's responses are an extreme form of resistance to human contact, with a concomitant extreme fascination and fixation on inanimate objects. Touching another person, expressing feelings, and relating to others are traumatic and largely avoided. Contemporary man is encapsulated in the world of his automobile, which may get more genuine concern and involvement than any human being in his life. Or, he is staring at his television, transistor radio plugged into his ear. . .a newspaper or magazine hiding his face, stimulated by liquor, cigarettes, and pills, aroused by pornography, eating frozen or pre-packaged foods, hitting golf balls at the driving range, and negotiating his life in two minute spurts over the telephone.

Significant relationships among humans require emotional expression and self-exposure. Emotions are not as easily integrated into male consciousness as they are into female consciousness. The factors that make emotional territory so terrifying to men are both natural and socially reinforced. A man's tendency toward abstraction is fueled by the underlying knowledge that he is excluded from the natural cycle. Emotions are associated with women, and the male aversion to things feminine often stifles the free expression of emotion. Much has been written about the social pressures that prevent males from channeling their emotions into the outside world, and many writers narrowly believe male inexpressiveness to be entirely a product of social influences. But advocates of social-learning theory should consider how sex-differences in the area of human interaction become apparent very early in life.

The primary focus of males and females is very different. Connection to others is the name of the game for females of all ages, even in their play. Dolls (the typical plaything of girls) are more conducive to intimacy training than the toy trucks and weapons boys get. You can cuddle a doll, comfort it, feed it, talk to it, sleep with it. But what can you do with a firetruck that has anything to do with relationships? (Zilbergeld 1992: 26)

Zilbergeld clearly understands and hints at the anatomical origins of sex difference but focuses on the more popularly accepted social aspects. When a boy shows his preference for a firetruck, a cap gun, or a model airplane over a doll or a teddy bear, he is unconsciously manifesting the increasing anxiety he has about proving his masculinity, to say that he is not a girl like his mother. As much as he may revere his mother for the essential care and life support she gave him, he knows on some level that the most critical tests of his identity will come not from the nurturing activities he associates with her, but from his performance in the outside world. Give a boy past the age of five or six a doll, and sooner or later, he will forsake it for something more action-oriented.

A frequent complaint women file against men is that they do not talk. Women seem perplexed at the male reluctance to share emotions, unaware of the true nature of the dilemma and its deep roots. Women's attempts to get men to communicate intimately can exert so much pressure that it is far easier for a man to terminate an otherwise promising relationship than plunge head-first into the dark, uncertain, and threatening world of emotion. This is tragic, perhaps, but understandable in light of the male condition. I do not mean to suggest that men should not attempt to become more at ease in opening up to their partners, or that intimate relationships are essentially unmasculine. But it is important to understand the tremendous disadvantage men have compared with women in opening themselves up emotionally in the way that is necessary for intimate communication. Of course, men do talk. But the quality of communication between human beings is very clearly influenced by the sex of the participants. Goldberg (1976:51) has one interesting and, I think, very truthful explanation for the frustrating male silences women report, specifically in conversations that have an adversarial quality.

Men are often silent, and their lack of communication is a common source of trouble in relationships. Most men exercise greater fluency in their conversations with other men. Discussion, debate and friendly arguments can go on for hours. But something peculiar happens when a man and a women converse, especially if there is an oppositional quality to the interaction. . . .Males learn early in life that they will lose any confrontation with a female, because win or lose they will be labeled "bullies." As a young boy he is castigated for fighting with his sister. He is taught that the female is fragile and that he is to be her protector, never her opponent or competitor. Her tendency to cry rather than to assert herself directly often results in a male reaction of guilt.

Any discourse between reasonably intelligent people is likely to reach a point of disagreement or contention, and most men carry with them an unconscious fear that their interactions with women will reach this point and that it will be impossible to emerge from a verbal skirmish with a female. Many women, often unaware that they are doing so, exercise their ability to express righteous indignation at male accusations of inaccuracy or faulty judgement, and in doing so can prevail in arguments by such default. While sex-differences in communication make themselves clear in the friendly academic debate between male and female co-workers, it is in the context of close relationships between men and women in which they become truly intense. With this in mind, let's investigate romance from a male perspective.

DATING

For young single men and women alike, the relationship arena has become a confusing one. Who asks out whom? Who picks up the tab? Sexual relationships, already fraught with anxiety and awkwardness, have become exceedingly convoluted. Women are certainly not immune to self-doubt and insecurity when it comes to their dealings with men. The image of the young woman fretting about what to wear on a date with a great guy, several outfits strewn about her bedroom while she looks at her body from every angle in the mirror, is a popular one. But men also endure agonizing uncertainties in the early stages of relationships. The ride home at the end of the evening on a first or second date is an emotionally critical time, when men and women's are often focused on very different thoughts. Herb Goldberg (1979:73) captures the essence of end of date-tension as experienced by men of all ages.

If he's still excited about her at the end of the evening, experiencing her as special, he might be looking for a sign that she is also attracted to him, be it through spontaneous holding of his hand, putting her head on his shoulder, or kissing him. If he is like most single men in our society, he is starving for affection, touching, intimacy and feedback that tell him he's lovable. . . .during the drive home he has to interpret her behavior. Is she sitting near the door (that means she is not turned on), or is she moving close to him (that means she likes him). Sometimes the signals are mixed and confusing and require acuity to interpret them. That is, she may be sitting close to him and yawning at the same time or she may be engaging in animated conversation while she sits tight up against the door. His signal reading activity better be accurate, because he is particularly vulnerable in the sexual arena. If he comes on to her and she responds with delight, then he'll be floating, suddenly transformed in his eyes into the most attractive man in the world. If she responds coldly however. . . .he will flood himself with self-hating messages and name calling. . . .Echoes of past accusations may then reverberate inside of him: "Horny! Insensitive! All you really want is sex!"

Reading women's signals is the most confusing part of new relationships for men. If women unconsciously yawn, laugh, or touch a man's arm on a date, the wheels in his mind are often spinning. A woman knows more or less when a man is attracted to her and so, emotionally and sexually, the relationship will progress at her pace. A man, on the other hand, must take risk after risk. He will ask her out knowing she may say no. He will hem and haw over the movie or the restaurant. He may initiate physical contact, knowing that if his timing or his assumptions are just a little bit off the mark, he will have not only embarrassed himself but perhaps thrown a relationship—whether pleasantly platonic or potentially romantic—down the drain.

Men today find themselves walking on eggshells when they approach potentially romantic territory with women. "Men are pigs" is a derisive generalization not one of us, in one form or another, has escaped. These insults resonate more strongly in our culture and in this era because we are strongly oriented toward the female sexual perspective: Women's attitudes are healthy; men's attitudes are defective. Because many women do not share men's feelings or fail to understand their origins, and because women currently hold the floor in the sex debate, such views are accepted without question and rarely rebuked.

SPORTS

Another aspect of daily life associated with men is sports. It is worth looking briefly at just how important sports can be as a conduit to male identity.

Boys who do not have what it takes to be successful athletes suffer intense feelings of inadequacy. Here, I think, social pressures make a significant mark. Fasteau reported in 1975 that only 5 percent of American fathers did not want their sons to be successful at sports. Although grown men themselves may not be athletically inclined, they realize the importance of prowess on the playing field in the emotional life of their sons.

Fasteau (1975:197) describes a man's negative recollection of a sports experience that illustrates the extreme pressure exerted on boys to develop athletic skill.

The father who pushes his son into sports with missionary zeal is so common as to be a part of our folklore. One man in his twenties, who described himself as having struck out more than any other nine-year-old on his little league team, told me that his father literally took him screaming and yelling to the games. . . .And when he did poorly, his father wouldn't talk to him for several hours after the game.

Even men who are not athletes, Fasteau tells us, identify with many elements of the sporting life:

In most spectator sports. . .qualities thought to be particularly masculine are at a premium: strength, speed, coolness under pressure, teamwork, the risk of violence, and the drive to win: then there is the satisfaction of a clear-cut decision—one team is a winner, the other a loser. Men understand and identify with these values and codes even if they are not athletes themselves. By devoted spectating and rooting, they vicariously affirm their membership in the club of certified males. (1974:108).

Men in all walks of life seem compelled by the mythology of sports and seek some of the associated glory. The locker room attendant, the towel boy, the team manager all belong to the throng who, although they may not be prepared physically or psychologically for the rigors of a game but want to be near enough to that special male in "hopes that the aura of masculinity will rub off on them" (Fasteau 1974: 109).

FRIENDSHIPS BETWEEN MEN

Special ties exist between heterosexual men. Close male friendships often have a quality that is not part of relationships between men and women or close friendships between women. Forming intimate relationships with other men presents unique challenges, but once established, intimate male friendships can also offer unique rewards.

In *The Death of the Heart*, Elizabeth Bowen (1948) wrote that "intimacies between women often go backwards, beginning in revelations and ending up in small talk without loss of esteem." Bowen unveils the central problem men experience when they cultivate friendships with other men.

In the progress of friendships between heterosexual men, a certain conflict may arise. A man may have a sincere desire to become closer to a another man, but fear that he will be perceived as threatening or at least unmasculine. He often tempers his outward expression of affection. Even two buddies who have known each other for years and have shared a wide variety of experiences only very rarely express their feelings toward each other or the important position each holds in the other's life. Love between men either goes entirely unspoken or is communicated in more subtle ways that do not upset the fragile male emotions.

Male-male friendships often grow in the context of a shared pursuit: sports, women, academic study, or any mutual interest. One man usually assumes a teaching role to the other, and this will eventually alternate as the relationship takes root. The common feeling of competition may contribute to male reluctance to exchange emotions. People in competition with one another do not naturally allow a competitor to take advantage of a vulnerability.

Of course, the male sense of competition has to be held in check if a friendship is to become intimate. It is probably not possible for two men to have a long-term close relationship without ever feeling as though they are in competition with one another. Success with women and income, when there is a great disparity between male friends, can stifle intimacy. Many an acquaintanceship does not become friendship because envy barricades the emotions. True friendship can arise when competition does not become a compulsion. It can even become a game. Less mature men, boys really, may outdrink each other or see who can get the most women into bed. Athletics are popular among many friendships that originate on the ballfield. Sports are based on healthy competition: Players admit they are in direct, heated competition with one another, and teammates form sturdy bonds in the pursuit of their common goal of winning the game. One team may win and the other lose, but good sportsmanship and a friendly handshake after the game are generally considered masculine because they demonstrate a man's ability to control his emotions. John McEnroe's tennis court tantrums do not draw the admiration of many men.

One final aspect of relationships between and among men is the feeling many women have toward male friendships. Women who are deeply involved in a relationship with a man may be distressed at his desire to spend time with his male friends. Women often do not realize that there is a nourishment men receive from other men which they simply can't provide, no matter how hard they try. It is reasonable to understand a woman's feelings of inadequacy in this situation. She may say to herself, "I give him everything I can. What does he get from his male friends that I cannot give him?"

Without question, both men and women need a variety of relationships at various levels of intimacy in order to maintain healthy social lives. A man's desire to spend time with one or more male friends separate from a wife or girlfriend is not an indication of the woman's inadequacy as a partner. Women who feel hurt by men sharing deep friendships with one another should take comfort in the fact that such unions make for healthier and happier men. Men who have the opportunity to develop special, strong bonds with other men are more likely to be stable, loving partners.

MEN AND WOMEN IN THE WORKPLACE

Work and economic success have been the primary yardstick of manhood in industrialized society. Although the working world is no longer the exclusive domain of men, We have seen that a feminist utopian vision of absolute job equity—gender balance at all levels of society and authority—is improbable due to inherent dispositions based in sexual physiology.

Let's turn away now from anatomical theory and history and focus on the emotions associated with men and work. In his exploration of masculinity *The Passions of Men* (1988), Mark Hunter explains the enduring bond between masculinity and work, which operates to some extent independently of social, political, and economic structures. While male inadequacy can lead to workaholism, the male orientation toward work is not altogether unhealthy.

Sooner or later a man gets a job, not just for the money, but because otherwise we do not consider him, in some essential way, a man. . . .In an even more essential way, he does not consider himself a man unless he works for money. That is not quite what a woman feels, as one might gather from reading advocates of post-feminist motherhood. . . .

They do not feel alright if they are not giving first rank in life to loving and being loved. [Men] have a relationship with work, a relationship as deep and satisfying, and in some ways unspeakably personal, as any other in their loves. In a real way, that relationship is sacred for men——as sacred as motherhood is for women. (Hunter 1988:110)

Hunter warns that we are making a serious mistake when we consider the possibility of men attempting to make relationships a bigger part of their lives. Hunter says we are not admitting a fundamental fact: "When you get right down to it, it is easier to be a success at a job than in one's human relationships." (1988:110)

One of the important changes the American male has been facing is the dearth of possibilities for all male achievement. This is, I daresay, more serious than the dearth of all male clubs and bars. . . .To the undying astonishment and regret of many men, there are few things in the United States today that American women do not or cannot do. They have invaded nearly all the formerly all-male occupational strongholds. . . .There are female sailors, tractor drivers, and carpenters, female pilots, telephone linemen, and lumbermen, female fishermen and locomotive engineers; even stevedores and longshoremen. . . .Why do I list the "manly" job categories which the ladies have infiltrated? Not to cause astonishment; not to mourn the passing of the all-male job world. I list them to emphasize that in America today it is no longer possible for men to affirm their maleness simply in terms of the tasks reserved for their side of the fence. (Brenton 1970: 81-82)

Some readers may be put off by Brenton's use of such words as "infiltrate" and "invade," but such words adequately reflect the psychological experience of men. For the most part, women see their growing presence in the formerly male-dominated job world as a victory, even if—or sometimes especially if—such gains are damaging to men's self-images. Women who feel this way have not adequately considered the implications of waning opportunities for men to discover and demonstrate their mascu-

linity. The most common view of the changing work arena goes
something like this: By eliminating the associations of certain jobs
with either men or women, both sexes will be liberated. Women
will gain independence and men will be free of their exclusive
responsibility as providers. It is also supposed that the introduction of a greater female influence into certain areas, such as
politics, will profoundly change the world order. One of the beliefs behind the argument for more women heads of state is that
such a change will mean a drop in military aggression.

Following Brenton, I raise this point not because I believe
women are less competent than men to perform the same jobs, and
not because I am necessarily nostalgic for the days when women
were confined to domestic duties, but rather to stress the importance of exclusively male tasks in a sound society. This assertion
is labeled conservative, though it merely reflects the historical and
anthropological evidence presented in Chapter 2. Men who do not
have specific male roles reserved for them will ultimately leave
the social environment or disrupt it with violence, crime, and a
general tendency toward sociopathic behavior. Because it seems
unlikely that the workplace will ever be strictly a male domain
again, men will inevitably search out new territory to call their
own.

THE APPEAL OF SEXUALLY EXPLICIT MATERIAL

Men consume erotic imagery far more frequently than women.
Some women express considerable discomfort with explicitly
sexual materials. Many more, while they may not take moral
offense at pornography, are at a loss to understand its appeal.
Generally speaking, women associate sex with emotional intimacy
more readily than do men, though men certainly are capable of
making this connection. I think it is safe to say that men have as
difficult a time *connecting* sexuality and emotional intimacy as
women do *separating* them. The romance novel or story appeals
to more women than men. Pornography allows men to engage in

sexual activity without risking emotional entanglement that would place them in a vulnerable position. Women clearly do not have the same general experience with the effects of sexual imagery, which is so powerful to men. Women, without question, find men attractive for physical reasons. But they are not subject to the same overwhelming feelings men encounter when assaulted by images of women's bodies. The feminist argument that pornography and erotic female dancers degrade women entirely overlooks the often hidden reactions of the men who view such photographs or attend striptease acts. Men are in awe. It is *they* who often feel powerless, while the dancers, who, significantly, dance on a platform above the men, exercise the power granted them by the mere fact of being born female. The image of the abducted teen-age drug addict forced to perform in sex shows or appear in pornographic films is a fantastic exaggeration; isolated incidents are dredged up to fuel feminist rhetoric. And economically speaking, the women are not exactly enslaved. Women who are the top dancers in clubs earn more in one night, perhaps $500 or $600, than many working men take home in a forty-hour week. Columnist and men's rights advocate Asa Baber (1992:159-160) takes to task the feminist notion of male oppression of women through sexual imagery.

When I look at Miss December I do not assume that she is a commodity for my consumption. . . .I do not envision her as a sexual slave, and in appreciating her shape and form or spirit, I do not degrade or humiliate her. I am simply a man who searches for beauty wherever he can find it. That does not make me a monster.

Recounting his youthful days gazing at the works of great art at the Chicago Art Institute, Baber (1992:159-160) proclaims the immutable visual nature of men's consciousness.

Look, it's simple, men love to look—you will never stop us, not even if you hang us for it. And if it ever does come to that, do me one last favor, will you? Make the job of hangman (hangperson?) equal opportunity employment. I wouldn't mind having someone nice to look at before she springs the trap.

FATHERHOOD

If becoming a father in the biological sense is one of the easiest tasks a man can perform, becoming a father in the truest, deepest sense is one of the most challenging. To say that motherhood comes naturally would be an oversimplification. Mothers come in many varieties and some are better than others. Some women will be better equipped, emotionally or physically, for child-rearing than others, depending on a complex interplay of circumstantial factors such as their own relationships with their parents. But the essential idea of what a mother is and does for her children seems more clear-cut than the role of the father. This may help explain the dangerous trend toward marginalizing the father in the American family. For every male the concept of fatherhood or the thought of becoming a father elicits mixed emotions.

Robert Bly (1990) stresses the father's crucial role in passing on appropriate models of male behavior to younger boys. Unfocused male energies are a potentially severe threat to our society which at present advocates a feminization of the family predicated on gender-feminist beliefs: Fathers are superfluous or expendable, therefore they are marginalized and given little incentive to remain in the home, especially among families at the bottom of the economic ladder.

Fully aware of the dangers latent in categorization, I have chosen to paraphrase the work of Ken Druck (1985), who classified fathers into seven groups, and named each with the defining traits of a certain kind of father. While such a system of classification is perhaps more appropriately employed by a botanist, Druck identifies some common positive qualities and pitfalls of fatherhood worth considering. Almost everyone will identify characteristics that describe their own fathering or apply to their father. Most will find that a father, whether it is they, their father, or fathers they know, are a complex mixture of these qualities, good and bad.

The seventh and final model of fatherhood Druck offers is an idealized version of a father. No father can expect to be the Loving-Present father all the time, but some offer something to strive for. No father should feel ashamed for having acted, at one time or another, like any of the other six characters listed. Neither should anyone pass too harsh a judgment on their own father for having displayed these common and very human characteristics.

The Admiral Dad

The Admiral Dad, in the truest sense, "runs" his family. He isn't likely to share in family activities because he's too busy making sure everyone is keeping to the schedule. Men who are raised in a home that operates like a tight ship under the command of the Admiral Dad reach maturity with a genuine respect for authority, but might lack an adequate model for such traits as emotional vulnerability, spontaneous behavior, and intimacy.

The Nice Dad

The Nice Dad sounds as though he would be ideal, and without a doubt he cultivates characteristics worth imitating. He is cooperative, patient, and sincerely concerned with the well-being of those around him. The Nice Dad, however, has difficulty setting limits. His need to please everyone stems from an inability to take emotional risks; his need for approval from others may outweigh his need to express his true feelings. As a result, he may be prone to outbursts of temper.

The Professor Dad

He's an expert on everything, and, to him, there is always only one correct way to do things. Children who grow up in a home with a Professor Dad often become perfectionists because they internalize the dad's critical voice, and may spend their adult lives seeking someone to tell them what to do all the time as a result of the dependence they developed on the Professor Dad.

The Sad and Mad Dad

The Sad and Mad Dad, according to Druck, "is deeply troubled and unhappy inside. He simply does not enjoy his life. But he never complains. Instead, he swallows his pain—that is, until he erupts into anger. The Sad and Mad Dad may inflict a burden of guilt on his children, who feel somehow responsible for his internal strife. With the Sad and Mad Dad as a model, children struggle with the repression of their own happiness and anger."

The Marlboro Dad

Responsibility, strength, and male power: The Marlboro Dad embodies success. "He's the first up in the morning and last to bed at night." He defines masculinity narrowly and traditionally as a form of absolute self-reliance and unbreakable constitutional stability. Here's what Druck (1985) says is the problem for the son of the Marlboro Dad: "He often sees his son as an extension of his own ego. He pushes hard for his son to become a success at school, in sports, with girls, and at work because it throws glory on his role as father. The son of the Marlboro Dad may opt for failure over success because that way he will not be in competition with a father whose act is impossible to follow."

The Hard-working Dad

As noble as it is to want to raise and provide for a family, the Hard-working Dad seems to have no other purpose. His exis-- tence revolves around supporting his family, primarily in the financial sense. He is not one to take after if you're seeking a healthy balance between work and play. The Hard-working Dad spends his vacations and off-hours guilt-ridden and restless, a trait he might pass inadvertently on to his sons. Stress usually compromises the physical and mental health of the Hard-working Dad and he is a good candidate for early death from heart disease or other stress-related illnesses.

The Loving-Present Dad

The Loving-Present Dad is like the 1950s TV father, who arrives home after eight hours at the office and appears refreshed, seeking friendly interaction with his family. He kisses his wife (on the cheek, of course) and expresses an avid interest in what the kids did in school that day. The Loving-Present Dad is a super- human myth, always patient and kind, never too busy for his fathering duties. He never worries about his children or money. Life is good to him and he just smiles. The Loving-Present Dad is non-threatening and almost sickeningly sweet. A little common sense should tell us that a good father is a model of behavior for his children, especially boys. A dad who never deals with the inevitable frustrations of life or demonstrates human short- comings would not be the best father because he would not be teaching his children how to deal with life's ups and downs.

The only identifiable mark of an ideal father is one who takes his position seriously, is more than fleetingly conscious of his tremendous responsibilities, and possesses the desire to be the best father he can be with what circumstance has given him. The best father is a man who has children because he expects that although his paternal role will be rough at times, a certain enjoyment will grow out of the energy he expends learning how to become a father.

As I close this overview of the interpersonal aspects of manhood, as well as the entire survey of men and masculinity, one word seems to be crucial: communication.

Men and women will always be at odds to some degree; the sexes will always be alienated from one another. But there is today a particularly divisive quality to gender relationships. To lessen the burden of sex-difference, men need to know as much about themselves as men as women know about themselves as women, and they must be permitted to study masculinity outside the tightening confines of feminist theory. Men will benefit by communicating their ideas, their needs, their reactions to women's changing roles, and the unique experiences they have simply because they are men to women and to other men. Dialogue on a personal level can lead to change in the greater community. Granted, men face problems of speaking as dissenters in the gender game because of the strong hold feminism has on our beliefs. But, as I stated at the outset, a number of books and media events in the last few years are evidence that a new, more realistic vision of men is surfacing. As they gather momentum, the phenomena known as the men's movement and men's studies will provide the challenge that feminism and women's studies require in order to become truly integrated components of gender studies. Perhaps a fresher, more balanced approach to human sex-difference, one that considers equally the nature of men and women, will light the way to a deeper understanding of humankind.

Appendix: A Statistical Portrait of Men and Gender in America

Unless otherwise noted, all data are from:

U.S. Bureau of the Census. Statistical Abstract of the United States: 1994 (114th edition) Washington, D.C., 1994.

POPULATION

U.S. Total, 1995:	263,434,000
Males:	128,685,000
Females:	134,749,000

Table 1: Males per 100 Females.

1995	95.4
1990	95.1
1980	94.5
1970	94.8
1960	97.1
1950	98.6
1940	100.7
1930	102.5
1920	104.0
1910	106.0
1900	104.4
1890	105.0
1880	103.6
1870	102.2
1860	104.7

Table 2: Males per 100 Females, by Age: 1992.

All ages	95.3
Under 14 years	95.3
14 to 24 years	104.3
25 to 44 years	99.2
45 to 64 years	92.5
65 years and older	67.8

HEALTH

Table 3: Average Life Expectancy at Birth by Sex and Race, 1850 - 1990.

Year	White Males	White Females	Non-white Males	Non-white Females
1850	38.3	40.5		
1890	42.5	44.4		
1920	56.3	58.5	47.1	46.9
1940	62.8	67.3	58.9	55.5
1960	67.5	74.1	61.5	66.4
1970	67.9	75.5	61.0	69.0
1980	70.8	78.2	65.6	74.0
1990	72.7	79.4	67.0	75.2

Table 4: Death Rates from Accidents and Violence, 1991.
(Deaths per 100,000 population)

Cause of Death	White Men	White Women	Black Men	Black Women
Motor Vehicle Accidents	24.4	10.8	25.6	8.7
All Other Accidents	23.3	12.6	34.2	13.5
Suicide	21.7	5.2	12.1	1.9
Homicide	9.3	3.0	72.0	14.2

ACQUIRED IMMUNE DEFICIENCY SYNDROME (AIDS)

Deaths 1982-1992:   166,467

Males: 148,863
Females: 17,604

Ratio of Male Deaths to Female Death from AIDS:

8.5 : 1

HEALTH INSURANCE COVERAGE

Percentage of Persons Not Covered by Public or Private Health Insurance, 1992.

Males: 16.5
Females: 13.1

CRIME

Table 6: Sex of Crime Victims, 1993.
(Rate per 1,000 persons 12 years of age or older).

	All Crimes	Rape	Assault	Robbery
Male	101.4	0.6	30.1	8.1
Female	81.8	0.8	21.1	3.9

Table 7: Handgun Crimes, 1993.
(Rate per 1000 persons 12 years of age or older).

Male	4.9
Female	2.1

EDUCATION AND EMPLOYMENT

Table 8: High School Diplomas Earned, By Sex.

Year	Men	Women
1900	38,075	56,808
1920	123,684	187,582
1940	578,718	642,757
1960	898,000	966,000
1982-83	1,437,000	1,451,000

Table 9: College Degrees Earned, By Sex.

Source: "The State of the Union." (Special Report) *Time*. 30 January 1995. vol. 145 no. 4. pp. 60-74.

	1972-73		1992-93	
	Men	Women	Men	Women
Bachelor's	56%	44%	46%	54%
Master's	59%	41%	46%	54%
Doctoral	82%	18%	62%	38%

Table 10: Percent of Women Who Work, 1973 - 1993.

Source: "The State of the Union." (Special Report) *Time*. 30 January 1994. vol. 145 no. 4 pp. 60-74.

1973:	45%
1980:	50%
1993:	59%

MARRIAGE AND FAMILY

Table 11: Median Age at First Marriage.

	Men	Women
1900	25.9	21.9
1920	24.6	21.2
1940	24.3	21.5
1960	22.8	20.3
1980	24.7	22.0
1992	26.5	24.4

Table 12: Percent of Population Never Married, 1992.

	Men	Women
20-24	80.3	65.7
25-29	48.7	33.2
30-34	29.4	18.8
35-39	18.4	12.6
40-44	9.2	8.4
45-54	7.3	5.3
55-64	5.6	4.0
65 and over	4.2	4.9

Table 13: U.S. DIVORCE RATE 1900-1992
(Rate per 1000 persons).

1900	0.7
1920	1.6
1940	2.0
1960	2.2
1970	3.5
1980	5.2
1992	4.7

Widows and Widowers: 1992.

Widows:	11,477,000
Widowers:	2,333,000

Unmarried Couple Households: 1992:   3,308,000

Percent with children under 15 years of age present: 34

Percentage of Births out of Wedlock to Women of All Races, 15-19, years of age:

65

Single Parent Households, 1990:

Male:	1,153,000
Female:	6,599,000

MISCELLANEOUS FACTS

Excerpted from: Tough, Paul. *What Counts: The Complete Harper's Index.* Edited by Charis Conn & Ilena Silverman; associate editor Paul Tough. New York: Holt, 1991.

Chances that a married working woman earns more than her husband:

1 in 5

Percentage of American women who said in 1970 that men were basically kind, gentle and thoughtful:

67

Percent who say this today (1991):

51

Chances that an American in 1975 thought that men had a better life than women:

1 in 3

Chances that an American thinks so today:

1 in 2

Estimated number of U.S. colleges and universities that offer courses in men's studies:

350

Estimated chances that an American couple married this year will get divorced:

3 in 5

Average duration of an American marriage before divorce, in years:

9.6

Chances that a white, college-educated, single, twenty-five year old woman will marry:

1 in 2

Chances that a white, college-educated, single, thirty-five year old woman will:

1 in 18

Percentage of cohabitating couples who were unwed in 1970:

1

Percentage who were in 1985:

5

Ratio of the number of divorce suits filed by women to the number filed by men:

2 : 1

Percentage of men who say they are happier since their divorce or separation:

58

Percentage of women who say this:

85

Portion of American families headed by a single parent:

1 in 4

Percentage of American households that consist of a father and children he is raising alone:

1.6

Percentage of American fathers who say they should share child-care equally with their wives:

74

Percentage who say they do share child care equally with their wives:

13

Percentage increase, since 1965, in the number of young married couples with children:

7

Percentage increase in the number without children:

80

Percentage of American children who live with two parents:

72

Suggestions for Further Reading

CRITIQUES OF FEMINISM

Gordon, John. *The Myth of the Monstrous Male and Other Feminist Fables*. New York: Playboy Press, 1982.

In this strong but lucid attack on feminist ideas, Gordon contends that the feminist movement is anti-sex and anti-male. He speaks for men who are displeased by the denigration of their sex and points to the hypocrisy of anti-male attitudes among feminists who speak for social equality.

Mailer, Norman. *The Prisoner of Sex*. Boston: Little, Brown, 1971.

This is one of the first significant critiques of radical feminism. Mailer severely criticizes Kate Millet's *Sexual Politics* and her interpretations of literary works.

PHILOSOPHY OF MASCULINITY AND GENDER

Fasteau, Marc Feigen. *The Male Machine*. New York: McGraw-Hill, 1974 (introduction by Gloria Steinem).

Fasteau was one of the first authors to question the damaging roles men assume in their quest for meaning and identity. He discusses competition, sports, violence, and friendships among men. Fasteau shares some perspectives with feminists, in that he sees androgyny as a solution to the growing rift between men and women.

Kriegel, Leonard. *On Men and Manhood*. New York: Hawthorne Books, 1979.

Kriegel offers a poetic account of his trial to discover his masculine identity after a childhood disease left him crippled. Kriegel praises traditional personifications of American manhood such as Ernest Hemingway and Marlon Brando, and dismisses the trend toward androgyny, which he sees as detrimental to both sexes.

Vilar, Esther. *The Manipulated Man*. New York: Farrar, Straus, and Giroux, 1972.

Vilar sees men as enslaved by women, and argues that women perpetuate a relationship between the sexes that reduces men to dependence on women. The author's version of the sexual economy is a system in which men support women financially in return for sex.

MEN'S RIGHTS

Doyle, R.F. *The Rape of the Male*. St. Paul, Minn.: Poor Richard's Press, 1976.

Doyle, who founded the Men's Rights Association, believes that favoritism toward women in contemporary society prevents men from receiving equal consideration under the law, particularly in divorce and child custody cases.

Schenk, Roy U. *The Other Side of the Coin: Causes and Consequences of Men's Oppression*. Madison, Wis: Bioenergetics Press, 1982.

Schenk examines the negative results of a society that he says oppresses men as much as women. He discusses anti-male attitudes of the feminist movement and counters the opinion that men are powerful oppressors and women helpless victims.

BIOLOGY AND PHYSIOLOGY

Hapsgood, Fred. *Why Males Exist: An Inquiry into the Evolution of Sex*. New York: William Morrow, 1978.

Peering into the scientific aspects of sex, this book offers an account of biological masculinity. Hapsgood explains four levels of sexual functioning in the animal kingdom, where humans belong to the highest group. The author talks about the specialization of sex roles, mating, and raising young, and finally, how love fits into the evolutionary process.

Rochlin, Gregory. *The Masculine Dilemma: A Psychology of Masculinity*. Boston: Little, Brown, 1980.

Rochlin's evaluation of a boy's need to establish his identity as separate from girls is an excellent introduction to the special needs of male children. Rochlin also provides a formidable literary interpretation of such classical works as Homer's epics and *Tom Sawyer* in terms of their usefulness in studying the condition of masculinity.

MYTHOPOETIC/SPIRITUAL

Bettelheim, Bruno. *Symbolic Wounds: Puberty Rites and the Envious Male*. New York: Collier Books, 1982.

Bettelheim presents puberty rites as attempts by males to imitate women's powers of procreation, comparing, for instance, the wounding of circumcision to female menstruation.

Harding, Christopher. *Wingspan*. New York: St. Martin's Press, 1992.

This title could be considered a comprehensive guide to the Mythopoetic men's movement. The text contains poetry, essays, drawings, and photographs about men and the spiritual approach to discovering manhood.

Jung, C.G. *Man and His Symbols*. London: Aldus Books, 1964.

This fully illustrated book explores Jungian theories of the human unconscious and the roles symbols and archetypes play in our psychology. This is an especially useful volume for those seeking a detailed explanation of the Anima and Animus concepts, which are central to the spiritual branch of the men's movement.

SEXUALITY

Hite, Shere. *The Hite Report on Male Sexuality*. New York: Alfred A. Knopf, 1981. Reprint. New York: Ballentine Books, 1982.

Hite's famous study was compiled from questionnaire responses submitted by over 7000 men, and includes interesting personal comments from respondents addressing such issues as pornography, marriage, impotence, and sex and the aging man.

Kinsey, Alfred. *Sexual Behavior in the Human Male*. Philadelphia: W.B. Saunders, 1948.

Kinsey's report, based on a sample of thousands of men, is the first scientific study of significance dealing directly with men and their sexual habits. Although it occasional seems dated, much of the information Kinsey includes is helpful today.

LITERATURE AND DRAMATIC WORKS

Clemens, Samuel Langhorne (Mark Twain). *The Adventures of Huckleberry Finn* (1884). Unwin Critical Library. Edited by Harold Beaver. Boston: Allen & Unwin, 1987.

This Twain classic presents perhaps the best integration of race and masculinity issues in an American fictional work. Huck, fleeing an abusive father, and Jim, as escaped slave, have something in common in that they are trying to resolve different but equally agonizing questions about their manhood.

Crane, Stephen. *The Red Badge of Courage* (1895). Edited by Sculley Bradley, et al. New York: W.W. Norton and Co., 1976.

A Civil War-era look at a young man's sudden confrontation with male identity in the context of combat. The protagonist, Henry, deserts his post during battle, then returns to claim the title of hero. One of the most salient themes in Crane's novel is his apparent questioning of the association of masculinity with war and violence.

Remarque, Erich Maria. *All Quiet on the Western Front* (1928). Translated from the German by Brian Murdoch. London: Jonathan Cape, 1994.

Patriotic slogans lure one young soldier into the German Army during World War I. The protagonist encounters the humiliation of rigorous military conditioning, only to be further dehumanized by the terrors of twentieth-century mechanized warfare. Having lost his companions in combat and emotionally battered by the constant strain of war, the main character's demise is presented by Remarque as a tragedy but also a relief.

Whitman, Walt. *Leaves of Grass*. Edited by Harold Blodgett and Scully Bradley. New York: New York University Press, 1965.

Whitman provides a variety of textual styles, ranging from prose to poetry to literary criticism, in this anthem of American masculinity. Most notable are Whitman's compelling thoughts on male emotional intimacy and companionship.

SOCIOLOGY AND ANTHROPOLOGY

Ehrenreich, Barbara. *The Hearts of Men: American Dreams and the Flight from Commitment.* Garden City, N.J.: Anchor Press/Doubleday, 1983.

Ehrenreich looks closely at the breadwinner role, which became obsolete during the 1950s and 1960s as the baby-boomer generation rebelled against corporate America and publications like *Playboy* promoted an image of the single life many men embraced.

Lee, Richard B. and Irven DeVore. *Man the Hunter.* "Symposium on Man the Hunter." (University of Chicago: 1966). Edited by Richard B. Lee and Irven DeVore. Chicago: Aldine Publishing, 1969.

A technical, in-depth study of the hunter role and its relationship to masculinity from an anthropological perspective. These academic essays were originally given in a symposium at the University of Chicago.

Mead, Margaret. *Male and Female: A Study of the Sexes in a Changing World.* New York: William Morrow, 1949.

Mead addresses one of the fundamental characteristics of masculinity: Society must allow channels through which men can express their manhood. Successfully arguing that girls are more secure with their identities than are men, Mead's greatest concern about the changing roles of men and women in the second half of the twentieth century is finding a way to teach men to desire children. Though Mead wrote her famous treatise on sex-difference almost twenty years before the modern women's movement, she opposes the notion that men conspire to oppress women and that women are the helpless sex.

Mitscherlich, Alexander. *Society Without the Father: A Contribution to Social Psychology* (1969). Translated from the German by Erich Mosbacher. New York: Harper, 1991.

Although difficult to access by those unfamiliar with Freudian theory, Mitscherlich's discussion of the paternal role in the development of young boys addresses critical issues of masculinity. When father absence from the home becomes a common feature of society, Mitscherlich contends, there will be profound effects on society and culture. This work strongly influenced Robert Bly's modern concept of Father Hunger.

Sexton, Patricia Cayo. *The Feminized Male: White Collars, Classrooms, and the Decline of the Male.* New York: Random House, 1969.

The author believes that the modern educational system is antithetical to the development of healthy masculinity. Sexton is particularly critical of the present-day society which rewards the typical behavior of girls but chastises boys for acting like boys. As a result of this arrangement in education, we are creating a feminized society in which men whom are the most masculine are unlikely to succeed. The ironic answer to the problem, according to Sexton, is the women's movement. When women participate fully in all social institutions, their influence on the domestic and educational environments will be less pervasive because men will no longer be, as she says, "targets of female resentment."

Bibliography

Amneus, Daniel. *Back to Patriarchy!* New Rochelle, NY: Arlington House, 1979.

Baber, Asa. *Naked at Gender Gap: A Man's View of the War Between the Sexes.* New York: Carol Publishing Group, 1992.

Bacon, Francis. *The Essayes or Counsels Civill and Morall.* Edited with an introduction and commentary by Michael Kiernan. Cambridge, Mass.: Harvard Unversity Press, 1985.

Baumli, Francis. *Men Freeing Men: Exploding the Myth of Male Tradition.* Edited by Francis Baumli. Jersey City, N.J.: New Atlantis Press, 1985.

Bliss, Shepard. "The Men of the Wound." *New Men, New Minds: Breaking Male Tradition.* Edited by Franklin Abbott. Freedom, Calif.: Crossing Press, 1987.

Bly, Robert. *Iron John: A Book About Men.* Reading, Mass: Addison-Wesley, 1990.

Bowen, Elizabeth. *The Death of the Heart.* New York: Knopf, 1948.

Brenton, Myron. *The American Male.* Greenwich, Conn.: Fawcett Publications, 1970.

Bullough, Vern. "On Being a Man in the Middle Ages." *Medieval Masculinities.* Edited by Clare A. Lees, with the assistance of Thelma Fenster and Jo Ann McNamara. Minneapolis: University of Minnesota Press, 1994.

Comte, Fernand. *Mythology.* Edinburgh: Chambers, 1991.

Denfeld, Rene. *The New Victorians: A Young Woman's Challenge to the Old Feminist Order.* New York: Warner Books, 1995.

Dimbleby, Richard, and Graeme Burton. *More Than Words: An Introduction to Communication.* New York: Metheun, 1985.

Druck, Ken. (with James C. Simmons). *The Secrets Men Keep.* Garden City, N.Y: Doubleday, 1985.

Ellis, John M. "Feminist Theory's Wrong Turn." *Academic Questions* 7, No. 4 (1994): 42-50.

Farrell, Warren. *The Myth of Male Power: Why Men Are the Disposable Sex.* New York: Simon and Schuster, 1993.

———. *Why Men Are the Way They Are: The Male-Female Dynamic.* New York: MacGraw Hill, 1986.

Fasteau, Marc Feigen. *The Male Machine.* New York: Dell, 1975.

Filene, Peter. "The Secrets of Men's History." *The Making of Masculinities: The New Men's Studies.* Edited by Harry Brod. Boston: Allen & Unwin, 1987.

Freedman, C. H. *Manhood Redux: Standing Up to Feminism.* Brooklyn, NY: Samson Publishers, 1985.

Friedan, Betty. *The Feminine Mystique.* New York: Norton, 1963.

Gaylin, Willard. *The Male Ego.* New York: Viking, 1992.

Gilder, George. *Sexual Suicide.* New York: Quadrangle, 1973.

Goldberg, Herb. *The New Male.* New York: Signet/New American Library, 1979.

———. *The Hazards of Being Male: Surviving the Myth of Masculine Privilege.* New York: Signet/New American Library, 1976.

Goldberg, Steven. *The Inevitability of Patriarchy.* London: Temple Smith, 1977.

Greenberg, Bradley S. *Life on Television: Content Analyses of U.S. TV Drama.* Norwood, N.J.: Ablex Publishing Corporation, 1980.

Greenstein, Ben. *The Fragile Male.* London; New York: Routledge, 1994.

Hawley, Richard. *Boys Will Be Men: Masculinity in Troubled Times.* Middlebury, VT: Paul S. Eriksson, 1993.

Henry, William A, III. *In Defense of Elitism.* New York: Doubleday, 1994.

Hoff-Sommers, Christina. *Who Stole Feminism?* New York: Simon and Schuster, 1994.

Hunter, Mark. *The Passions of Men: Work and Love in the Age of Stress.* New York: G.P. Putnam's Sons, 1988.

Iannone, Carol. "Is There a Women's Perspective in Literature?" *Academic Questions* 7, No. 1 (1993-94): 63-76.

Jeffords, Susan. "The Big Switch: Hollywood Masculinity in the Ninties." *Film Theory Goes to the Movies*. Edited by Jim Collins, Hillary Radner, and Ava Preacher Collins. New York: Routledge, 1993.

Keen, Sam. *Fire in the Belly: On Being a Man*. New York: Bantam Books, 1991.

Keillor, Garrison. *The Book of Guys*. New York: Viking, 1993.

Kilmartin, Christopher T. *The Masculine Self*. New York: MacMillan, 1994.

Kipnis, Aaron. *Knights Without Armor: A Practical Guide for Men in Search of the Masculine Soul*. Los Angeles: St. Martin's Press, 1991.

Kupers, Terry A. *Revisioning Men's Lives: Gender, Intimacy and Power*. New York: The Guilford Press, 1993.

McQuail, Denis. *Mass Communication Theory: An Introduction*. 3rd ed. London: Sage Publications, 1994.

Mellen, Joan. *Big Bad Wolves: Masculinity in the American Film*. New York: Pantheon Books, 1977.

Middleton, Peter. *The Inward Gaze: Masculinity and Subjectivity in Modern Culture*. London: Routledge, 1992.

Mitscherlich, Alexander. *Society Without the Father: A Contribution to Social* Psychology. New York: Harper, 1991.

Moore, Robert, and Douglas Gillette. *The Warrior Within: Accessing the Knight in the* Male Psyche. New York: Morrow, 1992.

Morgan, David H. T. *Discovering Men: Critical Studies on Men and Masculinities*. London: Routledge, 1992.

Ong, Walter J. *Fighting for Life: Contest, Sexuality and Consciousness*. Amherst, Mass.: University of Massachusetts Press, 1989.

Paglia, Camille. *Sexual Personae*. New Haven, Conn.: Yale Univesity Press, 1991.

Pangborn, Ken. "Confessions of a Men's Right's Activist." *Men Freeing Men: Exploding the Myth of the Traditional Male*. Edited by Francis Baumli. Jersey City, N.J.: New Atlantis Press, 1985.

Rosen, David. *The Changing Fictions of Masculinity*. Urbana, Ill: University of Illinois Press, 1993.

Rotundo, Anthony. *American Manhood: Transformations in Masculinity from the Revolution to the Modern Era.* New York: Basic Books, 1993.

Schoenberg, B. Mark. *Growing Up Male: The Psychology of Masculinity.* Westport, Conn: Bergin & Garvey, 1993.

Smith, Richard Keith. "Television and the Male Image." *Men Freeing Men: Exploding the Myth of the Traditional Male.* Edited by Francis Baumli. Jersey City, N.J.: New Atlantis Press, 1985.

Stearns, Peter N. *Be a Man! Males in Modern Society.* New York: Holmes & Meier, 1990.

Thomas, David. *Not Guilty: The Case in Defense of Men.* New York: Morrow, 1993.

Thompson, Keith. "An Interview with Robert Bly." *New Men, New Minds: Breaking Male Tradition.* Edited by Franklin Abbott. Boston: Allen and Unwin, 1987.

Tiger, Lionel. *Men in Groups.* New York: M. Moyars (Distributed by Scribners), 1984.

Upton, Charles. *Hammering Hot Iron: A Spiritual Critique of Bly's "Iron John."* Wheaton, Ill: Quest Books, 1993.

Vanderburg, William H. *The Growth of Minds and Cultures: A Unified Theory of the Structure of Human Consciousness.* Toronto: University of Toronto Press, 1985.

Wilson, Glenn D. *The Great Sex Divide: A Study of Male-Female Differences.* Washington, D.C.: Scott Townsend Publishers, 1992.

Wright, Robert. *The Moral Animal: The New Science of Evolutionary Psychology.* New York: Pantheon Books, 1994.

Zilbergeld, Bernie. *The New Male Sexuality.* New York: Bantam Books, 1992.

Index

About the Author

STEPHEN WICKS received his MA in Media and Communication from New York University.

ISBN 0-89789-454-5

90000>

EAN

9 780897 894548

HARDCOVER BAR CODE

WITHDRAWN